The Crucified and Resurrected Method of Living the Recovered Life

"To help readers achieve the greatest possible clarity and understanding in their reading of the text of the Amplified Bible, some explanations of the various markings within the text is necessary: Parentheses ( ) signify additional phrases of meaning included in the original word, phrase, or clause of the original language. Brackets [ ] contain justified clarifying words or comments not actually expressed in the immediate original text, as well as definitions of Hebrew and Greek names" Quoted from the introductory text of the Amplified Bible

Spaces inbetween the paragraphs of the Crucified and Resurrected Method of Recovery are left intentialy for personal notations and journaling. The reader is encouraged to write down his or her thoughts regarding the daily reading.

To my beautiful wife Cheri

DAY ONE

Admitting that you are in sin

  Sin is rebellion against the law of freedom which being in Christ Jesus provides. It can easily progress into an addiction and addiction is a bondage to a sin pattern. Admitting to an addiction can be a good thing in a sense that it is a breaking down of the denial that often surrounds the problem. Admitting that you are in sin and "addicted" is the first step in recovering from that addiction or sin. This is obviously necessary. However, the downside is that through this admission we may come to think that this is who we are at the core of our being. Nothing can be further from the truth for the born again believer.

  If we are born again the truth about who we are in Christ has been established. Christ established our identity through what He did at the cross. It will help us to renew our minds to the facts of what happened there . We became a new creation in Christ. We can admit to our problems but that alone will not help us. Our study of what happened at the cross will help us walk in the reality of "I am crucified with Christ nevertheless I live". Again, it will require study.

  If we are born again we are first and foremost children of God. We have been recovered spiritually from a fallen state and have been restored into a state of completion. The realization of this state of completion comes through our dependence on the blood of Christ which was shed at His cross. The blood of Christ washes away all our sins and perfects us. The truth is we have already been set free in Christ. Understanding what Christ has already done for us there will give us the psychological, and social awakening we need experintially. Christ's coming to this earth and dying for us is the means of this regeneration.

A child of God can get caught up in addiction and find that they are in bondage to sin. We don't choose the bondage consciously. We made a bad decision and were deceived into this bondage. Much damage has been done and healing can take some time for us. This healing will be found at the foot of the cross. At the cross we find the love of God. God's love is expressed through what He did for us there. He replaced our selfish heart for His caring heart.

Jeremiah 23: 28-29 "The prophet who has a dream, let him tell his dream; but he who has my word, let him speak my word faithfully. What has straw in common with wheat [for nourishment]? Says the Lord. Is not my word like fire [that consumes all that cannot endure the test]? Says the Lord, and like a hammer that breaks in pieces the rock [of most stubborn resistance]?"

Journal

DAY TWO

Our belief and decision

Living the cruciformed and resurrected life is living a life of eliminated self reliance "through" what Christ did at the cross for us. It was there that the "old man" we were was completely put to death. We can fall back into "self reliance" through unbelief in what Christ did for us at the cross. We need to admit when we fall back into self reliance lest it progress to self will run riot. Self reliance is self centeredness and is to be avoided at all cost. That cost is the cross of Christ. When we admit to self reliance we can take it to the cross by faith and exchange it for Gods care for us that was offered there. It is there that our will is put to rest and we are given His will for us. His will for us is that we participate in the reality and meaning of His resurrection and ascension into the heavenly realm. We are risen with Him!

We choose to experience living the resurrected life through our belief and decision. But we must also know what Christ has done for us regarding our sins. We are not to ignore our sins, shortcomings and character defects. There is a death involved in dealing with them. This death occurs previously to living this resurrected life. That is the death of the old man we use to be at Christ's cross. All of our sins, shortcomings and character defects are leftover faults that exist in our "flesh" from the old man we once were. By "flesh" I mean a self centered effort at living this life which excludes Christ. "Flesh" is easily activated by self reliance

We are instructed to "cast all our cares upon the lord". This is obviously something we need to practice as we place our faith in Christ's work.. Placing our faith in Christ is a fight we are called to. His finished work included several truths that are essential to our understanding and can not be overstated. God recreated us and when we place our faith in Him we experience this new creation. He put to death the old person we use to be and created in us a new person. It was at the cross that He met all our spiritual, psychological, and social needs. It is through His blood that our "will" is properly exchanged for His will. Our decisions and choices to trust what God has done for us through Christ's death and resurrection will be ongoing. This decision is no mere technique for it is based on fact. It is based in the fact that our life has been exchanged for His life at the cross.

Our decisions and choices are necessary but they are not exactly what changes us. Our decisions and choices are used to accept what God has done for us. When we make these decisions and choices of "heart surrender" we find that God has already met our needs. He does better than that. We find that God starts doing for us what we could not do for ourselves on our own. He takes care of us. Although it is our will that initiates choice and complete dependency on Him it is through union with Him that He works out His will in us. At first we will not recognize Gods action within us. With a little time we will begin to see how God works in spite of ourselves. We will see that we have actually begun being a carrier of God's will.

We can do so much introspection that we can become overfocused on our shortcomings and our "self" at the expense of the cross. However we must weigh in the blood content of Christ, His death, and resurrection for us. That "weighing in" is our cross to bear. This will keep us balanced as we consider ourselves. It is very important to allow God to supervise our introspection process. Anything outside of Gods leading in this area will probably be insignificant and a waste of time. We need a deep rooted understanding of "God's part" is in our lives. When we fully understand what God has done for us as Christians it makes it easier to "Let go and let God" and to "Turn it over" to Him.

Corinthians 4:8-10 "We are hedged in (pressed) on every side [troubled and oppressed in every way], but not cramped or crushed; we suffer embarrassments and are perplexed and unable to find a way out, but not driven to despair; We are pursued (persecuted and hard driven), but not deserted [to stand alone]; we are struck down to the ground, but never struck out and destroyed; Always carrying about in the body the liability and exposure to the same putting to death that the Lord Jesus suffered, so that the [resurrection] life of Jesus also may be shown forth by and in our bodies."

Journal _____

_____

_____

_____

_____

_____

_____

DAY THREE

Regeneration and recovery

You will only be hurting yourself if you do not take advantage of Christ's finished work. It is His blood alone that cleanses and perfects us. Due to Christ's work at the cross we are regenerated. That means that we have received new "genes". Recovery for the born again Christian is regaining in our experience what was given to us by God and taken from us by satan through deception. Recovery for the Christian usually includes much more than we originally had before satan took it from us.

In the book of Romans the Apostle Paul stated "I was alive without the law once but when the law came sin revived in me." This "alive without the law" was the freedom that Paul found in Christ initially when he was born again. Then the enemy came and stole that freedom from him by deceptively imposing the law of scripture. Through the Apostle Paul's self effort to keep these laws he lost his freedom. Paul concluded that his freedom is found in Christ alone. Recovery for us means that we rediscover that initial born again experience plus more. We learn how to allow God to deliver us from the law that satan has brought into our lives. Recovery for the Christian is different than recovery for the non-Christian. The non-Christian doesn't have the born again regenerated experience as a baseline. However, salvation is available to everyone! If you don't know Christ you can ask Him into your heart now!

Everything that I am speaking about here is in Romans 6, - 7, & 8 of the Holy Bible. Have you as a Christian studied these three chapters? It's not rocket science and is written in a way that can be understood. Dysfunction is a symptom of attempting to live by the law under the steam of our own self effort. But we have been set free by the Spirit of life in Christ Jesus. Our character defects are faults that appear when we place our trust outside of our freedom in Christ.

Our faults are our sins. There is no nice way to put it. Character defects are sin. Sin is what was laid on Christ when He was crucified. All sin. It is not we who bear these sins and bury them. It was Christ. His blood washed away all our sins past, present, and future! Our part is to appropriate our lives to what happened when we were crucified, buried and re-surrected with Christ. It was at the cross that the sin issue was dealt with completely.

God has nothing to do with character defects. It's not what He created in us. He doesn't make faults. So why spend year after year living under the law and focusing on our defects? God loves us and we have value in spite of our occasional failures. Sometimes the rebellion of the "flesh" (self- effort) gets the best of us. Understanding the blood of Christ and His love found therein helps us to relate to ourselves. The revelation of His care for us is known through an understanding of what He did for us at the cross. It is then that we are ruled by love. It comes through the cross. God is love and His love for us is expressed through Christ crucified for us.

Romans 7: 9-11 "Once I was alive, but quite apart from and unconscious of the Law. But when the commandment came, sin lived again and I died (was sentenced by the Law to death).And the very legal ordinance which was designed and intended to bring life actually proved [to mean to me] death. For sin, seizing the opportunity and getting a hold on me [by taking its incentive] from the commandment, beguiled and entrapped and cheated me, and using it [as a weapon], killed me."

Journal

DAY FOUR

Finding the solution in our groups and gatherings

It's good to to have a place where we can gather together with other Christians who have found a way to live in the Lord. It's also good that we have a place to gather with others whose lives have been torn apart by addiction and have been put back together. It is good to find a group that accepts us as we are and gives us a sense of belonging. We need a place where we can know others and be known. We need a group where everyone shares their struggles and how they are finding solutions to their problems. A group where the great gifts of the Spirit abound and it is like the church God has intended His church to be. Those of us who have been regenerated from such a terrible state have much to share from our experience.

The Christian "backslider" or the addict is not alone. Groups exist so that people can find their solution in Christ and the power of His shed blood! However, groups alone will not improve our lives. Only the person of Jesus Christ and His cross does. Therefore any good group will point to this fact. It will establish itself and stay consistent with the true gospel. It's not a group and Christ. It's not Christ and a group. It's a group that points to Christ. And not just Christ but his finished work done for us as well!

Christian groups are made simple by a group of regenerated people who have found and share a solution which is in Christ. The solution is sanctification. Sanctification means to live by the operation of our baptism into Christ unto holiness. We carry to our groups the truth of how Christ's cross has changed our life. We share how the finished work of the cross can be applied to our everyday struggles. At first this kind of sharing may seem strange and misunderstood. As time goes by people will grow accustomed to this kind of sharing. But it does go against "worldy" advice giving.

Attending groups is a learning experience for us. As we get acquainted with our group of brothers and sisters in Christ we become more honest with one another. We stay with those who the Lord has assembled us with. It is there that we learn about Christ and share the ministry gift that God has given us! No one person in the group is more important than another. Even the leader of the group is just a servant. God wants us all to grow in the expression of his word!

Hebrews 3:12-14 "[Therefore beware] brethren, take care, lest there be in any one of you a wicked, unbelieving heart [which refuses to cleave to, trust in, and rely on Him], leading you to turn away and desert or stand aloof from the living God. But instead warn (admonish, urge, and encourage) one another every day, as long as it is called Today, that none of you may be hardened [into settled rebellion] by the deceitfulness of sin [by the fraudulence, the stratagem, the trickery which the delusive glamor of his sin may play on him]. For we have become fellows with Christ (the Messiah) and share in all He has for us, if only we hold our first newborn confidence and original assured expectation [in virtue of which we are believers] firm and unshaken to the end."

Journal

DAY FIVE

A child of God or an addict?

I remember when I first started going to recovery groups some 30 years ago or so. I struggled with the idea of introducing myself as an addict or an alcoholic. I often thought to myself "this is a bad confession". When I finally got clean in 1995, I was so beat up that I would have siad anything I was told to say. So I went along with the program and introduced myself as an alcoholic and an addict.

After many years clean I started to think "I am more of a child of God then anything else". One thing I can state 100% for sure is that I have a history of addiction. I know what it means to give everything up for that drug. I know how it feels to walk the street homeless and hopeless.

Calling ourselves children of God while at the same time calling ourselves addicts can be confusing. One is a statement of who we are and the other is a statement of what we do, or have had a propensity to choose to do. We live in a society that tends to identify what we do with who we are. So we hear things like "I'm a doctor" or "I'm a truck driver".

We also identify with conditions in our society and hear things such as "I'm a diabetic" or "I'm bipolar". So it is no surprise that the same thing happens when a person has an addiction problem or a sin problem. The person admits "I'm an addict" or "I'm a sinner". However, addiction is not who we are. It's a component of a type of behavior we engage in or have engaged in habitually.

Isaiah 38:17 "Behold, it was for my peace that I had intense bitterness; but You have loved back my life from the pit of corruption and nothingness, for You have cast all my sins behind Your back."

Journal

_____

_____

_____

_____

_____

_____

_____

DAY SIX

Addressing Immoral traits

Having better morals will be a symptom of the Spirits move in our life but that should not be our focus. On the other hand a lack of faith in God results in immoral behavior and is a pretty good indicator that we do not trust the Lord. Don't get me wrong, we remain responsible for our behavior! However, the "way" of controlling our behavior "on our own" is not to be our focus. Jesus stated that He was "the way". We must always depend on the lord. This dependency is not a passive dependency. It is a conscientious choice that we make throughout the days and events of our lives. This dependence upon what the Lord has done for us on the cross needs to be weaved into all our believing, choosing, and sharing. Otherwise we run array in our own self efforts and we will not live the resurrected life.

We do not solve our problems by focusing on our problems We solve our problems by focusing on the solution to our problems. Immoral traits are only symptoms of distrust and can not be dealt with by addressing them directly. Satan's ploy is to get us to focus on and live by morals. He maneuvers in ways to get us thinking that we can fix ourselves. In this way he takes us away from the cross and the resurrection of Christ as the solution on how to live this life. Satan then places further attention on manipulating us into a "self reliant" effort to live right. But, we are not to live "by" morals anymore. We are to live by the Spirit. And there is a big difference between the two. Trying to live by morals is an attempt to produce our own character. Living by the Spirit is allowing the fruit of the Spirit to manifest in our character What must be dealt with is our trust in the Lord. He then will manifest "fruit" in our character and lives.

We who come to Christian Bible studies or Christian recovery groups have been in the church for a very long time! Now is the time for us to move off of "milk" and get on to some maturity. We can't allow ourselves to sit in these seats year after year without change. I am challenging you to study Romans 6, 7, & 8! I am going to give a little preview of these chapters as follows. In Romans Chapter 6, The Apostle Paul shows us what happened to us spiritually with Christ in His crucifixion, burial, and resurrection. Then in Chapter 7, Paul uses himself as an example to show us what happens if we try to live this Christian life under our own power. Romans Chapter 7 teaches us that our main focus should not be on attempting to live by morals by focusing on morals alone. We will see how the Apostle Paul tried over and over to do right and could only do wrong. Then in Romans Chapter 8, Paul shows us that we should focus on yielding to the work of the Spirit in our lives as previously discussed in Romans Chapter 6. In this way we will manifest the fruit of the Spirit. It's not as complicated as it seems.

Romans 8: 1-3 "THEREFORE, [there is] now no condemnation (no adjudging guilty of wrong) for those who are in Christ Jesus, who live [and] walk not after the dictates of the flesh, but after the dictates of the Spirit. For the law of the

Spirit of life [which is] in Christ Jesus [the law of our new being] has freed me from the law of sin and of death. For God has done what the Law could not do, [its power] being weakened by the flesh [the entire nature of man without the Holy Spirit]. Sending His own Son in the guise of sinful flesh and as an offering for sin, [God] condemned sin in the flesh [subdued, overcame, deprived it of its power over all who accept that sacrifice]"

Journal

DAY SEVEN

Truth does not negate sin

Yes it is true that we are new creations in Christ and that God has broken the power of satan's evil, the world's evil, and sin in our lives. However, these truths don't negate the need to admit to sin when we do sin. If we see that we are resting on our own laurels and are caught up in sin we own up to it. We also see and consent to our own powerlessness. These admissions just become side notes as we face what Christ has done at the cross to correct our dilemma. Our focus is not to be centered on useless self effort but on what God has done to end these sinful flesh patterns. We understand that sinful flesh has its roots in the satanic and contributes to our psychosocial disturbances. It also has its roots in a self governing effort that excludes what Christ has done for us.

These symptoms of sin can be traced back to what we can call "our part" which will always manifest an indifference and lack of faith in God. This is where satan will try to bump into our self examination and impose condemnation. Here is where we need to understand that there is no condemnation to those who are in Christ! Yes, there will be failures on our part which are a result of self effort. But we need to remember that God still loves us. We can apologize to God for our lack of trust in Him in various areas of our lives. This apology benefits us mostly for the Lord is all understanding and compassionate. Even though we sin we still have great opportunity to grow and have a deeper relationship with the Lord!

An examination of our lack of faith is oftentimes neglected when we do a personal inventory. We should look at our offensive behavior and what in our life feels threatened. We should look at "our part" in how we handle what threatens us or causes us to be in fear. We can always include a lack of trust in God on "our part". This lack of trust is many times driven by fear. However, if we factor in "God's part" it will make all the difference in our personal inventory. Understanding and seeking "God's part" in our inventory is of utmost importance. God gives us peace. He has established some realities within us that we may have sat on the back shelf of our heart and neglected.

These realities need to be brought to the front of our personal inventory and sat upon the main display case of our lives! We need to break through our denial and accept the fact that God has put to death the person we were and raised us into new life. Once we break through the denial and accept who we are in Christ we can begin to take advantage of the good life God has provided for us. The facts of what Christ has done for us at the cross must no longer be disregarded. We have taken on His life and His will because we have been baptized into His death and His resurrection. We find a new path to walk planted in our hearts. Now that's what we can call an inventory! Let us inventory accordingly.

1 John 1:9 "If we [freely] admit that we have sinned and confess our sins, He is faithful and just (true to His own nature and promises) and will forgive our sins [dismiss our lawlessness] and [continuously] cleanse us from all unrighteousness [everything not in conformity to His will in purpose, thought, and action]."

Journal

DAY EIGHT

Amends and accountability

Much of what this life is has to do with is getting our social needs met. God wants to meet our need in this area. He wants to be involved in our social relations with others. He also wants us to turn to Him to get our needs for acceptance and self worth. Satan also comes to us in the social area as well. He wants us to get our social needs met through some of his ways. What could those ways be? They will be in the way of eliciting self centered defensiveness or offensiveness. It may not be easy to forgive the terrible hurts that we suffer or to forgive ourselves when we inflict pain on another but the cross will make the difference. The work of the cross separates the sin from the person who committed the sin.

That is where the forgiveness of God is found! We no longer have to tie this sin to the person who has sinned against us and we no longer have to be bound to the sins that we commit toward others. This goes for every sin from mild neglect to the severe.

When another person angers us and we are about ready to speak our mind the Lord tries to step in and say "I've got this one" Of course we need to be open to the Lord in order for Him to do this. We need to take a time out and understand what God says about forgiveness in His word. We can decide to be obedient to His word by trusting in the work of the cross. Since Christ has separated the believer from his sin through the cross we too can separate our view of our associates from their sin! I believe that this is exactly what the Apostle Paul was doing when he addressed Christians as "saints" in his letters. He was coming from the view of the cross. But was he passive in dealing with sin? No.

God is not vindictive but he does hold the Christian accountable. He convicts the believer of sin. He encourages us to lean on His strength to overcome it. His strength is expressed at the cross. We realign ourselves with the victory won there over satan and the fact of the creation of a new man in us. This trust on our part is our responsibility. We live by faith. We find purity in our lives as a result of His shed blood!

1 Peter 3:8-9 "Finally, all [of you] should be of one and the same mind (united in spirit), sympathizing [with one another], loving [each other] as brethren [of one household], compassionate and courteous (tenderhearted and humble). Never return evil for evil or insult for insult (scolding, tongue-lashing, berating), but on the contrary blessing [praying for their welfare, happiness, and protection, and truly pitying and loving them]. For know that to this you have been called, that you may yourselves inherit a blessing [from

God--that you may obtain a blessing as heirs, bringing welfare and happiness and protection]."

Journal

___

DAY NINE

We don't live off of our "accountability"

I have been around the rooms of recovery for most of my life. I have been in and out of many drug and alcohol programs as well. I am also a Christian. So it is no surprise that I talk about the things I have experienced. And yes certain ideas were presented to me on how to live a spiritual life through the years. There are certain perspectives that I feel the Lord would have me share.

One area is the concept of the removal of sinful character defects. I have learned that substituting the words "character defects" in place of the word "sin" should be an area of caution on our part. It is a term that seems to make our sins more acceptable. God accepts us fully but He does not accept sin! Should we? If we think we can continue in sin and have the grace of God it could mean that we really have no grace at all!

You will always come up with sinful character defects and shortcomings when you are preoccupied with yourself. Admit your sin and move on. Get over it! Instead, become occupied with Christ's forgiveness that flows from the cross. We can become occupied in a good way with the new creation that came through Jesus' death and resurrection. We can rest in Christ's finished work.

Being restless is a sin. God gives us just enough account-ability to exercise our will to make a decision of faith. This is called in scripture a measure of faith. However, we don't live off of our "accountability". There is not enough in our "account" and it will leave us bankrupt. Accountability lies with the Lord and He has made a way for us through His cross. There is no need to crucify ourselves. That puts the focus on us. We were already crucified with Christ. That puts the focus on Him.

Philippians 2:12-13 "Therefore, my dear ones, as you have always obeyed [my suggestions], so now, not only [with the enthusiasm you would show] in my presence but much more because I am absent, work out (cultivate, carry out to the goal, and fully complete) your own salvation with reverence and awe and trembling (self-distrust, with serious caution, tenderness of conscience, watchfulness against temptation, timidly shrinking from whatever might offend God and discredit the name of Christ).[Not in your own strength] for it is God Who is all the while effectually at work in you [energizing and creating in you the power and desire], both to will and to work for His good pleasure and satisfaction and delight".

Journal

DAY TEN

Choosing to act on belief

Believing is simply accepting what is true and choosing is to act on that belief. Believing and choosing is not easy to do for some. Some people have trouble with the the idea of letting the God of the Bible into their Life. But we as Christians gladly accept Him. After admitting to and confessing to our addictions we need to learn to trust in the Lord again. Our path is now turning out of denial and into practical solutions for our lives. We now believe that our lives are in the hands of the Lord. Now that we are in the hands of the Lord we are making a decision to continue in the faith. We are now deciding to live this life the way the Lord wills us to.

Everything that we are was created through Christ's blood, death, resurrection and ascension. The reason we "decide" is due to a belief in the expression of Gods love toward us. This choice bears down on what Christ did for us at the cross. He put to death the old man we were and created in us a new man. A decision for the Lord that doesn't consider Christ crucified and resurrected could just be a wasted choice. God is giving us a choice so that we can place it in Him and the reality of Christ's finished work. It is the blood alone that saves us and provides for us a path to walk. It is all rooted in His love. We are His children and we are dependent upon that love. We respond to that love

Fully understanding what happened for us at the cross increases our insight into His love for us and builds up our belief in God. It was at His cross that He unified Himself with us in love. He is pure love. He is the only authentic source of Love. We know no love without Him. So we respond by believing in Him and making a decision to turn our lives over to Him and His love. Christ's finished work includes the new person He created in us along with satan's complete defeat in our lives. We reap the benefits of Christ's finished work at the cross.

It is God who works in us to choose to take advantage of the benefits of the cross. We accept the changes that happened to us when Christ accomplished what He came to this earth to accomplish. That is to shed His blood for our cleansing. It is through Gods gentle persuasion that we make this choice to believe in the power of this shed blood. But God never pushes His will on us. The challenge for Him is "our will". The challenge for us is to say "Thy will be done". We can be joined to Him! The reason we have a will is so that we may place it in Him and what Christ did at the cross.

2 Peter 1: 3-4 "For His divine power has bestowed upon us all things that [are requisite and suited] to life and godliness, through the [full, personal] knowledge of Him who called us by and to His own glory and excellence (virtue). By means of these He has bestowed on us His precious and exceedingly great promises, so that through them you may escape [by flight] from the moral decay (rottenness and corruption) that is in the world because of covetousness (lust and greed), and become sharers (partakers) of the divine nature."

Journal

DAY ELEVEN

Our groups reacquaint the Christian with the Lord

People just don't stumble into our Bible studies or recovery groups. Many show up because they are experiencing some kind of crisis that their addiction or sinful lifestyle has created. Because of the intensity of their problem, and the psychosocial instability involved, the newcomer is always the most important person in the room. People who have addictions and whose lives are overrun with sin are looking for those who can help them out of their dilemma. We must be ready to deliver a solution!

We as a group have the opportunity to intervene in this person's life. We must not be so involved in the drama of our own lives, or the life of the group, to the degree that we overlook the newcomer's needs. The correct action is to be led by the Holy Spirit. As members of Christ's body and as group members we should always be in a "state" of carrying His message. We keep in mind that the newcomer in our group is a person with real needs.

We as "old-timers" share that we can not free ourselves from addiction by focusing on the addiction. We share that we can't fix the damage we have done by attempting to fix it all on our own. Our confession is that it takes somebody way bigger and much stronger than us to do this. We share that we trust in the lord and the powers He destroyed at the cross. As we did this "trusting" our areas of concern lined up with the

Spirit of God. Addictions were broken and relationships were healed.

This is the overall purpose of why we meet. We meet to share and grow in these truths. We give all the glory to God! As we consider our confession of who we are in Christ we can take into account how we relate it to others. Explaining our spiritual position in Christ can be helpful for both us and others. We explain specifically what Christ has done for us. We also explain that Christ has done it all for us and that He will continue to provide. We confess that nothing is impossible to the Lord. With this in mind we can approach others without demands and with the peace of God

2 Corinthians 5:16-18 "Consequently, from now on we estimate and regard no one from a [purely] human point of view [in terms of natural standards of value]. [No] even though we once did estimate Christ from a human viewpoint and as a man, yet now [we have such knowledge of Him that] we know Him no longer [in terms of the flesh]. Therefore if any person is [ingrafted] in Christ (the Messiah) he is a new creation (a new creature altogether); the old [previous moral and spiritual condition] has passed away. Behold, the fresh and new has come! But all things are from God, Who through Jesus Christ reconciled us to Himself [received us into favor, brought us into harmony with Himself] and gave to us the ministry of reconciliation [that by word and deed we might aim to bring others into harmony with Him].

Journal

DAY TWELVE

Letting go of our own efforts

There seems to be some confusion over the definition of character defects. Character defects are simply sins. We have learned that to live this life for God we have to own up to our sins and believe in God to experience the forgiveness of that sin. Sin is Sin. By not addressing it we are hurting ourselves. We have to admit that when we reject Christ, we sin. Rejecting Christ is THE sinful character defect and shortcoming that births all other sinful character defects and shortcomings. It is a very ugly and stomach turning act. There is no other way to look at it.

We STOP rejecting Christ and we admit that we are powerless to change our life on our own. We stop rejecting Christ by yielding to Him and through accepting His power. The only solution for sin is the cross and what happened there. This needs to be more commonly taught. Many teach us behavior modification techniques on how to live a Holy life. However, the blood of Christ alone can make us stronger than we ever could imagine ourselves to be experientially. But Christ within us is the source of that power.Cognitive and behavioral modification fails by comparison.

If we could have removed our character defects we would have done so long ago. But we have now reached the point where we are now entirely ready to experience the power of God. Nothing less can free us. So we are brought to a point. That point is to experience the power of Christ through our crucifixion, burial, and resurrection WITH HIM. Think about that the next time you are tempted to sow to the "flesh" or act out in your own efforts. We can no longer devalue what Christ has done for us.

Christ died unto sin at the cross. If we want God to remove our character defects we must accept this fact. There is no other method that we can take that will remove our shortcomings. We do not generate goodness on our own. We do not generate evil either. We are either under the power of evil or under the power of God. The choice is ours. Because we are identified with Christ in His death we can be dead to sin experientially through our faith in His finished work. The complete work of Christ doesn't just remove our character defects. It created a new man within us. But it's faith in the power of His shed blood, His resurrection and not in ourselves that brings God's power.

Romans 5:8-10 "But God shows and clearly proves His [own] love for us by the fact that while we were still sinners, Christ (the Messiah, the Anointed One) died for us. Therefore, since we are now justified (acquitted, made righteous, and brought into right relationship with God) by Christ's blood, how much more [certain is it that] we shall be saved by Him from the indignation and wrath of God. For if while we were enemies we were reconciled to God through the death of His Son, it is much more [certain], now that we are reconciled, that we shall be saved (daily delivered from sin's dominion) through His [resurrection] life."

Journal

DAY THIRTEEN

Communication skills

In this life there will be times that we will act out in sin and that will cause hurt and anger in others. It could be anything from an unkind word on. Others will sin against us as well. If we are offended it may be a symptom of our pride and distrust in God. The Holy Spirit will not involve Himself with the building up of our ego. He never needs to defend Himself from the actions of others because everything He found offensive was taken care of at the cross! Christ sat unfamiliar boundaries with others when He was carrying His cross and being crucified. He stated "Father forgive them they no not what they do".

It is by understanding Christ's love that we can see His love for others. It has nothing to do with improving our social skills. Improving our communication skills many times encourages self reliance. It's about God using us to share His love. When God's love comes through communication is an automatic. The love of God for those around us is not of our making. Our attempt to "Love" can only interfere with His love for He is love. His love is beyond our attempts to have successful relationships. The only adjustment we need is to His love.

It is only through the cross that our sins and the sins of this other person have been dealt with. We learn to see ourselves and other Christians as being "in Christ" regardless of our psychological state or social behaviors. The answer is depending on Christ and His love. Then His love will come through. Our part is to be open to the revelation and adjust to it through yielding. On the other hand we deal as the Lord leads in regards to offensive acts. The Love established for us and in us at the cross is able to withstand the "bombs" delivered by satan toward us through others.

This doesn't mean that we stay unequally yoked to those who are habitually abusive. God may guide us out of abusive relationships. We may find out that we are the abuser and that we are the one who needs to stop. Nevertheless, the blood of Christ flows freely from God to all. God is the source of love. No matter how much hatred is expressed toward us it is our responsibility to do as Christ did. He took it to the Father. He forgave. He still does. He does it through us. This is the "greater works" that we do according to His word. When we trust what He did for humanity we automatically and with desire follow His command to love.

2 Corinthians 2:14-15 "But thanks be to God, who in Christ always leads us in triumph [as trophies of Christ's victory] and through us spreads and makes evident the fragrance of the knowledge of God everywhere, For we are the sweet fragrance of Christ [which exhales] unto God, [discernible alike] among those who are being saved and among those who are perishing"

Journal

30

DAY FOURTEEN

Inventory, admission, and forgiveness

Self reflecting without a bearing on what happened to us at the cross of Christ reveals nothing spiritual and can just be a waste of time at best. As we do our fearless moral inventory we look within at the inner workings of morality or lack of morality. Immoral behavior is sin. Our sins are only indicators that we are engaged in a "flesh pattern" or if you like to call it "living by our own will under the power of our own effort". A flesh pattern is a way of living that we learned from the old man that we were before we accepted sanctification.

A "flesh" pattern is made up of sin. It is living independently of God. A study of our flesh patterns may not be necessary in our inventory but it is at least worthy of some examination. We may need to just admit that it is there and admit to the damage we have caused others as a result of it. We then can place our minds on that which is above and from the Lord. This prevents what is called "morbid self reflection". It would please satan if when we inventoried we only placed our focus exclusively upon ourselves. This is a trap.

When we inventory ourselves and we find sin we admit to it, thank God for His forgiveness, ask others for their forgiveness, and turn our inventory over to examine our union with Christ at the cross. What Christ did for us at the cross was absolutely necessary for us to recover from living in our addiction and for us to be restored back into a relationship with God. Look to the cross! Our self absorption ends there. We need to place our mind on the spiritual realities God placed in us. We want to live a moral life by the Spirit of God.

The fruit of the Spirit will meet our moral obligation. When we discover within us "flesh patterns" the temptation is to attempt to modify these flesh patterns. The problem is that these flesh patterns can not be modified in a way that pleases the Lord. We need to be able to distinguish between our own self effort which is of the "flesh" and the empowering of the Holy Spirit which first includes our faith in the crucifixion of our flesh by Christ. This faith is a blind spot for many Christians. Let us open our eyes to the whole truth about who we are.

James 5:15-17 "And the prayer [that is] of faith will save him who is sick, and the Lord will restore him; and if he has committed sins, he will be forgiven. Confess to one another therefore your faults (your slips, your false steps, your offences, your sins) and pray [also] for one another, that you may be healed and restored [to a spiritual tone of mind and heart]. The earnest (heartfelt, continued) prayer of a righteous man makes tremendous power available [dynamic in its working]. Elijah was a human being with a nature such as we have [with feelings, affections, and a constitution like ours]; and he prayed earnestly for it not to rain, and no rain fell on the earth for three years and six months. [I Kings 17:1.]"

Journal

DAY FIFTEEN

Denial and acceptance

We as Christians have our Lord Jesus Christ and His shed blood to believe in for our recovery and restoration. But it requires us to take off our blinders and admit to our sins to take advantage of the freedom Christ paid for us at the cross. We must cut through self deception to get a good view of what has been happening in our lives. So we admitted to our sins. Sins can become strong habits that can hold us in bondage. It is a habit that is formed on our rejection of the redemptive work of Christ in our lives. Sorry, but there is no easy way to put it.

Our object of "addiction" or selfishness only offered us temporary moments of pleasure. There were promises of satisfaction but the payoff was always condemnation and ruin. When we thought of turning to the Lord satan would offer "solutions" to our dilemma. He attempted to get us focused on ourselves to find our own solutions. Some of these fixes looked very religious. He would use scripture to form law to keep us from grace. He knew that if he could keep us focused on ourselves that we would continue in our addiction.

The reason why satan attempted to get us to control our addictions and our lives is that he was hoping that he could destroy us. Satan threw everything he had to throw at us. We were no less than a slave in our selfishness and in our attempt to fix ourselves. We admit to consenting to the foolish tactics that satan used on us. We admitted to ourselves that we fell into addiction. We admitted to ourselves that we had deep trust issues and thus turned outside of the Lord for comfort. We admitted that we didn't believe that the Lord could meet

ALL our needs. We had to face the hard facts to rid us of any denial. And it was the lord that brought us to this point.

After we moved out of denial we needed to understand that we were born of God. This is what we needed to learn over again. God has planted in us His incorruptible Spirit. We began to understand again that our salvation and even our daily walk is a gift from God. He has provided for us His blood and His body. His blood was given for the penalty of our sins. His body was given for our new life through His death and resurrection. The only person to believe in is Jesus Christ and the only thing to believe in is what He did for us at the cross. The problem was we were not accepting Gods power until we found it in our relationship with Christ.

Romans 7:17-19 "However, it is no longer I who do the deed, but the sin [principle] which is at home in me and has possession of me. For I know that nothing good dwells within me, that is, in my flesh. I can will what is right, but I cannot perform it. [I have the intention and urge to do what is right, but no power to carry it out.] For I fail to practice the good deeds I desire to do, but the evil deeds that I do not desire to do are what I am [ever] doing."

Journal

DAY SIXTEEN

Recovery and being recovered

I've tried many things to improve my life throughout the years. I've read an endless amount of self help books covering almost every topic as it regards self and how to relate to others. Now as I look back over the years and upon my personal library I can see that none of these writings helped me very much at all. God knows I've tried to apply the suggested techniques. The funny thing is, out of all these books, no matter how sweet the cover, they never mentioned the death, burial, and resurrection of Christ as the solution.

Just changing my thoughts to be a better person did not work for me. I was hard on myself when it came to character development. I had to learn that a good life lived is through the fruit of the Spirit and those fruits do not come about through my own self effort. They develop as I trust in God's redemptive work for me. My own rational-emotive capability to live this life is bankrupt and can not be trusted. On the other hand, I never new that this life could be so good. I only have God to thank. He is the Man behind my peace.

As I go along in this life my choices to turn to Him seem to be getting easier and easier. Yet, if you were to look at my life you might think "This is only an ordinary person with ordinary problems" But, if you could have seen where God has brought me from you would without a doubt say "This is a miracle!" In my recovery process I have done several things. I have admitted to having sin in my life, I have come to believe that the Lord could restore me, and I have made the choice to let Him.

All of this responsibility of admitting, believing, and choosing still left me in the driver's seat focused on me. My focus needed to come off of myself and onto the Lord. It's not all about me. So I kept in mind that it is none of these things that grant me Gods grace. This admitting, believing, and choosing, is only a response to Gods love. It is only His cleansing blood that restores me. In Him I am completely recovered in Christ! The reality is He chose me! I was chosen and changed before the foundation of the world.

Ephesians 1:7-9 "In Him we have redemption (deliverance and salvation) through His blood, the remission (forgiveness) of our offenses (shortcomings and trespasses), in accordance with the riches and the generosity of His gracious favor, which He lavished upon us in every kind of wisdom and understanding (practical insight and prudence), Making known to us the mystery (secret) of His will (of His plan, of His purpose). [And it is this:] In accordance with His good pleasure (His merciful intention) which He had previously purposed and set forth in Him"

Journal

DAY SEVENTEEN

Our most valuable "stock"

I worked a system of "personal inventory" for years and there was some truth to it. This personal inventory had me get to my part in my "psychosocial" disturbances. "My part" always constitutes getting defensive when my psychosocial instincts are threatened. For many years I was leaving out "God's part" in sanctifying me. The truth is Christ's finished work at the cross is my most valuable "stock". Every other item is valueless without it. I look at my dependent state and see that it fits perfectly with God's strength. Seeing the reality of the death of my sins in Christ allows me to experience freedom from sin!

Admitting our sins, and bringing them to the work of Christ, ends our involvement with sin! The power and glory of the effects of the cross are within us! They are freely given to us by God and are a part of us. We hand it all back to the Lord! There is a spiritual battle that surrounds us when we do a personal inventory. Satan will do anything he can to divert us from our focus on the cross and the destruction of the our sinful nature that happened there. Satan's battle is to keep us focused on the sinful flesh and on self effort as if the cross never occurred. God wants us to know that our self reliant efforts to live for Him negate the work of the cross. Our own self reliant effort will equate to sin every time.

We can generate a list of sins and take them back to God. But this list will only benefit us because it addresses our denial. Due to the shed blood of Christ, God remembers our sins no more. God desires faith not a list of character defects and shortcomings. It is through faith that we willingly give up our whole life and allow God to express His power in the way He wishes to through us. We can ease our minds and give up our deep and dark analysis! We can gain perspective and an understanding of what Christ crucified means to us.

We are no longer who we use to be and the power of our own efforts was broken on His cross. The thinking that we must depend on our innermost selves must change into the accepting of God's life in us. There is a vast difference between the two. Our salvation and sanctification does not depend on our capacity. Our innermost self is not capable. Truth is given by revelation through God. It comes from accepting what Christ did for us at the cross and the meaning of His shed blood. Then the truth is revealed and lived through us. We need to do an examination of our faith in the truth above all things.

1 Peter 1:18-20 "You must know (recognize) that you were redeemed (ransomed) from the useless (fruitless) way of living inherited by tradition from [your] forefathers, not with corruptible things [such as] silver and gold. But [you were purchased] with the precious blood of Christ (the Messiah), like that of a [sacrificial] lamb without blemish or spot. It is true that He was chosen and foreordained (destined and foreknown for it) before the foundation of the world, but He was brought out to public view (made manifest) in these last days (at the end of the times) for the sake of you."

Journal

DAY EIGHTEEN

Topics for group discussion

Isn't it great to have a place where we can go that is interactive and based in the love of God! It's in our gatherings that we share the hope we have found. Each individual will have their own experiences to share in regards to their growth in Christ. Overall we share that we trust Christ to take care of all our needs. We share that we needed to let go of our own hold on our lives. We share that we can trust Christ to take care of our social issues and psychological well being.

We share that we place our faith in what Christ did at the cross to straighten us out! Our sharing confirms our understanding of who sets us free. We share that there is nothing that we did to experience the freedom we have in Christ. That freedom is given to us as a gift through the work that Christ finished at the cross. We share that our own efforts did not earn us this freedom. The only effort that was required of us was to place our faith in Christ and what His shed blood has done for us.

Others in the group will hear what sets us free and in turn will be encouraged as well. So we share our insights. We share how we have learned that it is our own efforts that make up the flesh. That "Flesh" equates to self effort. We share how we've learned that our recovery is not about our own efforts and that we are not to battle our flesh on our own. We make it clear to the group that we've found that our battle does not take place in the flesh but in the spiritual.

Our whole mindset refocused itself on the spiritual battle that was won for us by Christ. By sharing what worked for us we are being of service. These groups are about discovering Christ. When we discovered Christ we "found ourselves". Again, we share how our focus is off of our self efforts and on the spiritual battle won at the finished work of Christ. Our efforts do not eliminate addiction and sin. Our confession is that these "powers" were destroyed at the cross.

2 Thessalonians 1:10 (Amplified Bible) "When He comes to be glorified in His saints [on that day He will be made more glorious in His consecrated people], and [He will] be marveled at and admired [in His glory reflected] in all who have believed [who have adhered to, trusted in, and relied on Him], because our witnessing among you was confidently accepted and believed [and confirmed in your lives]."

Journal

DAY NINETEEN

Moving relationships toward healing

Emotionally injuring others through a bad attitude or neglect is a sin whether we want to admit it or not. Our sinful character defects are rooted in rebellion against what Christ has done for us at the cross. It is only the finished work that was done by Christ that can eliminate them. Our stubbornness is what holds on to them. When we understand this we are more inclined to surrender to the work of His shed blood. Now we can see how this same truth applies to others.

The scriptures teach us to be tolerant and long suffering with others. Knowing that Christ dealt completely with everyone's personal issues at the cross allows us to be patient and kind. As we anchor ourselves in the Lord the Holy Spirit will move through us to be an example to those He has put into our lives. We are incapable of doing this on our own. We can only allow the Spirit to move us into obedience. This happens as we understand and claim the finished work of Christ in our own lives.

In regards to our relationships we are responsible to turn them over to the Lord. If we take them into our own hands we can make a mess of them. What makes us think that we can fix them? Our relationships are in need of an intervention. This intervention will be done by the Holy Spirit as we trust God to have His way in our relationships. Surrendering it all to the Lord is always "our part". Not having our eyes fixed on the Lord in regards to our relationships will get us in trouble every time.

We can't fix our relationships by ourselves. We need the Holy Spirit to speak to our hearts and guide us in our interactions with others. The Lord will adjust our eye sight in regards to our relationships. Anger is many times felt by someone when something is not fair. All of us are quick to claim this unfairness. It is only through Christ's cross that these burdens we put on each other can be tolerated. We need to remember that all of us dish out our burdens. We do not always love and neither do others. Love can only be fully realized in Christ's shed blood.

1 John 1:7-8 "But if we [really] are living and walking in the Light, as He [Himself] is in the Light, we have [true, un-broken] fellowship with one another, and the blood of Jesus

Christ His Son cleanses (removes) us from all sin and guilt [keeps us cleansed from sin in all its forms and manifestations]. If we say we have no sin [refusing to admit that we are sinners], we delude and lead ourselves astray, and the Truth [which the Gospel presents] is not in us [does not dwell in our hearts]."

Journal

DAY TWENTY

If at first you don't succeed die die again

We must depend on a power and an action taken outside of ourselves and that is Christ crucified and resurrected for us. When we are not identifying with who we are in Christ it is no surprise that we do not reflect His character. What we will reflect during those times are own efforts. We need to allow our thoughts to be changed by the power of God. Through an appropriate inventory of self we can examine our faith. Our faith is what will make the difference. It is important that we inventory our capacities IN Christ.

When our inventory reveals our own efforts we are tempted to attempt to modify these efforts. The problem is that these efforts can not be modified in a way that pleases the Lord. We need to be able to distinguish between our own self effort which is of the "flesh" and the empowering of the Holy Spirit which first includes our faith in the crucifixion of our sinful flesh by Christ. We are dead to sin. This is a fact. We will have to come to experience that fact many times in our lives. This faith is a blind spot for many Christians. God allows circumstances to occur that will open our eyes to the truth.

Our work is to seek and respond to an understanding of how God operates. What the Holy Spirit does for us is He points out areas in our lives where we fall short of faith and then He guides us into the truth. That truth will always be Christ and what His shed blood means for us. We in turn take our shortcomings back to the Lord, admit to them, apologize and then the Holy Spirit points to the finished work of Christ and our resurrection with Him.

Our shortcomings of faith are always of our own making through very bad choices resulting in character defects. That which is not of faith is sin. Belief, decision, and accountability factor into God's inventory of us. Is it there? Are we making decisions that are lining up into an agreement with God? Are we "letting go" of the process of controlling our own lives? Is there abandonment there? Are our lives and decisions turned over to Him? Do we know that it is in Him that we live? Are we 100% dependent on the finished work of Christ?

Hebrews 13:12 "Therefore Jesus also suffered and died outside the [city's] gate in order that He might purify and consecrate the people through [the shedding of] His own blood and set them apart as holy [for God]."

43

Journal

_____

_____

_____

_____

_____

_____

_____

DAY TWENTY ONE

Pride

It is our pride that needs to be baptized into Christ death. It is the Holy Spirit Himself that humbles us enough to accept this fact. It is only when we accept this fact that the Holy Spirit is able to manifest authentic peace in and through our lives. Peace when it is promoted by pride requires effort and always fails. It is through our baptism into Christ's death that we die to sin.

Christ is magnified not just through our life in Him but through our death in Him. By death I mean death unto our old man and death into areas of our life that we can't even reach or even see on our own. Baptized into his death = crucified. Baptized into his life = resurrected. This is the way God operates to bring about change in our lives. It is through the destruction of the power of the flesh and the death of the old man that we were that propelled into spiritual resurrection.

Unbelief keeps us tied to our character defects and shortcomings. We do not generate the fruit of self control in regards to our behavior. It is generated by belief in the Holy

Spirit as we place our faith in the power of the blood of Christ. We do not bring the fruit of faithfulness to the work of God. It is brought by the Holy Spirit as we place our trust in the finished work of Christ. We do not "perform" the fruit of goodness in regards to other people. It is performed by the Holy Spirit as we place our faith in our co-crucifixion and resurrection with Christ.

We can do nothing apart from Christ and what He did for us at the cross! When we understand and trust in how the Holy Spirit operates we will be more open to HIS character. This will greatly reduce our character defects. When we rely on ourselves the outcome will always be shortcomings. This is why we stay dependent on God and the blood of the lamb. Personal obedience comes through the fruit of faithfulness. It is a gift!

Colossians 2:12-14 "[Thus you were circumcised when] you were buried with Him in [your] baptism, in which you were also raised with Him [to a new life] through [your] faith in the working of God [as displayed] when He raised Him up from the dead. And you who were dead in trespasses and in the uncircumcision of your flesh (your sensuality, your sinful carnal nature), [God] brought to life together with [Christ], having [freely] forgiven us all our transgressions"

Journal

DAY TWENTY TWO

We came to believe who we were in Christ

We can see that the principle of conversion is a gift. To see it we have to go back to where Christ shed His blood. What happened there is God established our identity. All our "issues" or sins were dealt with when He said "It is finished". We were crucified and resurrected with Him. We only needed to have the action that was already done for us to be brought up to date. This was absolutely needed for our experience of regeneration. After we came to believe who we were in Christ we had a better view as we looked back upon our addictions and their consequences in our lives.

Now we can see our life for what it is. In the past we were engaging in unbelief. We didn't think the Lord could meet all our needs. We trusted something else to bring us pleasure. That something else became a vice. We became addicted to a wrong way of living. We were deceived and bound by satan. Our addiction grew to the point that it threatened our very lives. As Christians we knew we couldn't continue on this way. Our whole belief system had to be rearranged to fit the Lords way of operating.

In our personal lives we came to know that believing without a bearing on Christ crucified and resurrected is believing that is wasted. This lack of proper belief stole from us our experience of who we were "in Christ". Through Christ's resurrection a new man was created within us. Through Christ's ascension a new man was also raised with Him. We were raised up above all powers! We were attached to Christ's body through His crucifixion, His death, His burial, His resurrection, and His ascension. Nothing can stand against that! So called Christian "beliefs" are only thoughts if they lack a dependence on the power of the blood of Christ!

Christ died unto sin so that we could be dead to sin. To experience being dead to sin is to rest in the reality of the finished work of Christ. We change by accepting what Christ has done for us! Let's not get caught up in focusing on ourselves. Let's get caught up in focusing on Christ and what He has done for us. Let's BELIEVE in what Christ did for us. We need to study and understand what Christ's crucifixion and resurrection means to us. Accessing what he did for us requires an understanding. We accept the fact that we need to come to terms with HIS solution for us. So we go back to the principle of the conversion we went through when we were born again.

Ephesians 2:13 "But now in Christ Jesus, you who once were [so] far away, through (by, in) the blood of Christ have been brought near."

Journal

DAY TWENTY THREE

We are delivered

If we don't understand the power of the blood of Christ how can we share our Christianity? We may think that we know about it and now we can move on. However, if we think we have grown beyond the need for the cross and the meaning of what happened there then more than likely we have slipped into "self righteousness". Walking in grace comes directly from the finished work of Christ into our day to day lives as we continue to abide in His burial and resurrection! And we do need to abide in Him daily. Knowing this, how could we not carry this message to our Christian gatherings?

In regards to deliverance are we telling people about the power of what happened at the cross? In regards to daily living are we experiencing and sharing the power of what happened at the cross? Let us fit the cross into all our living ! Let us fit the cross into all our sharing. Lets find contentment in its meaning. Let us let it's message consume us. The old man that we were has been put to death there! The new man that we are is found there! It is in Him that we can live moment to moment throughout the circumstances of our lives.

Our existance as Christians depends on the ongoing power of what was established on Christs cross and the work that was done there. Are we giving this truth the appropriate amount of time in our group Bible studies and interactions with others? Why not? What happened at the cross of Christ defined His care for all of us. When we fully understand what happened when Christ was crucified and make that the focal point in our lives it gives us a healthy perspective. Our baptism into His death, burial, and resurrection give us all the assurance we need to have our needs met.

If we don't carry this message we are in danger of embarking on a program of personal works. When we lift up Christ and what he did for us at the cross the Holy Spirit sends who He wills to hear it. It is His love that sends others to us. It's all about soul surgery. But the operation must be performed in the way God orders it! Since we as individuals have experienced His life we are able too pass it on to others. It is His message on how we are changed that we pass on.

1 Corinthians 15:56-58 "Now sin is the sting of death, and sin exercises its power [upon the soul] through [the abuse of] the Law. But thanks be to God, Who gives us the victory [making us conquerors] through our Lord Jesus Christ Therefore, my beloved brethren, be firm (steadfast), immovable, always abounding in the work of the Lord [always being superior, excelling, doing more than enough in the service of the Lord], knowing and being continually aware that your labor in the Lord is not futile [it is never wasted or to no purpose]."

Journal

DAY TWENTY FOUR

If we say we have no sin

We can be fooled into thinking that we are being led by the Spirit when in reality we are not. So we need to test the spirits. To test the spirits we need to weigh the "blood content" of the ideas being presented to our mind and the amount of emphasis that is put on the cross. By blood content I am referring to what Christ did to regenerate us. The blood of the cross should be evident in our perception of Christianity. Is this being made abundantly clear in our thinking? When Christ said "It is finished" He didn't just mean that He was done paying for our sins. He also meant that He was done putting to death the old man that we use to be. He also made us dead to committing future sins. It took His shed blood to accomplish this task done for us. That's love. But it's up to us to respond to His shed blood. That response is what is meant by "carrying our cross". It may take some revelation but if you seek for it you will find it.

If we say we have no sin the truth is not in us. But Christ died unto sin. If we have our faith placed in Him we too are dead to sin! Then through His resurrection life He becomes our righteousness and holiness. If any degree of holiness could be achieved through our own personal effort then Christ wouldn't have had to come and die for our sins. Self reliance burrows deep into the character of a man. Only the blood of Christ can expose it and flush it out! Our union with Christ is the sole purpose of this life and our union with Him can be perfect because He is perfect. May you find this in your personal inventory.

We can take what I call the "Romans 6, 7, & 8 test". We can ask ourselves questions such as these "Am I experiencing enough unmanageability and desperation in my life to meditate on the truth of these chapters? If not am I complacent?" If I answer "Yes" to the second question then this complacency must be dealt with. We won't go through our life without sinning. But for the most part we can. God promised us that sin wouldn't dominate our lives. However, taking advantage of that promise requires faith in the finished work of Christ. Do you not see yourself as you are? God created us new creations in Christ.

Does not the Holy Spirit see us when we sin? If not how can He convict us and move us away from it? God observes sin and the price paid for it is Christ crucified. He is not blind. He has removed our sin as far from us as the west is to the east! To experience that separation we need to have faith in what happened at the cross. Our thoughts and actions must be laid aside. We are not perfect but we can grow to the point that we too can say "I am not here on my own accord. I am here to believe what the Holy Spirit instructs me to believe" From that point on we must be sure that what we believe is the will of God. From there the challenge is the step of faith.

Romans 6:10-12 "For by the death He died, He died to sin [ending His relation to it] once for all; and the life that He lives, He is living to God [in unbroken fellowship with Him]. Even so consider yourselves also dead to sin and your relation to it broken, but alive to God [living in unbroken fellowship with Him] in Christ Jesus. Let not sin therefore rule as king in your mortal (short-lived, perishable) bodies, to make you yield to its cravings and be subject to its lusts and evil passions."

Journal

DAY TWENTY FIVE

Christ's cleansing blood made us new men

Self examination is not easy. A moral inventory is a look at right and wrong conduct. It takes a sharp eye and skill to understand what exactly we are looking at when we examine ourselves. The word of God is the lens through which we can get a close view. We are interested in the morals that are rooted in the "Spirit". But when we examine ourselves and see our immoral behavior we understand that these wrongs are rooted in unbelief.

Our bad "stock" always has this unbelief attached to it. We see that unbelief has opened us up to be driven by fear in certain areas of our lives. We see that being driven by fear has psychological and socially damaging components. We look at the choices that are causing this damage. Unbelief and bad choices ultimately factor into the damage done. Immoral behavior is usually just a symptom. However, if we have harmed another making an amends is in order.

We need to understand that God performed spiritual surgery on us at the cross. His blood has made us new. His finished work is our restoration! That is why Christ came to this earth. It is at the cross that He removed our heart of stone and replaced it with a heart of flesh. "Our part" is to decide to place our faith in this fact. This faith in Him is a response to His love and the shed blood that completed His operation on us. It's not so much self care as it is allowing God to care for us. We don't do surgery on ourselves.

Self care has become very familiar to us and is something that we have held on to tightly in our lives. Self care has failed us. We found out that self care was just a nice way to frame our selfishness. This self care in many ways plays into a flesh pattern (self effort) that we have learned from the old man we use to be and from this evil world. A flesh pattern is simply a survival technique of one form or another.

Inappropriate self care, self reliance, self centeredness and self determination are not Gods way for us. They are worldly principles and they lay wasted at the cross. What we experience is God's care through our co-crucifixion, and resurrection with Christ.

John 3:15-17 "In order that everyone who believes in Him [who cleaves to Him, trusts Him, and relies on Him] may not perish, but have eternal life and [actually] live forever! For God so greatly loved and dearly prized the world that He [even] gave up His only begotten (unique) Son, so that whoever believes in (trusts in, clings to, relies on) Him shall not perish (come to destruction, be lost) but have eternal (everlasting) life. For God did not send the Son into the world in order to judge (to reject, to condemn, to pass sentence on) the world, but that the world might find salvation and be made safe and sound through Him."

Journal

DAY TWENTY SIX

Releasing judgment and anger

Others can frustrate us and place stress on us but if we retaliate we only have ourselves to blame. This response is not Godly and we need to admit this. When we have reasons to judge others the reasoning and judging becomes our problem. When we blame others for anything we are usually excusing ourselves from being loving. We need to trust God with this other person. God is in control. God loves this person He has placed into your life.

The reasons for judging others becomes our own problem to own. This other person is in the hands of God and God is working on them to bring them fully into the new person He wants them to be. The person who offends us is in the hands of Christ. It is "our part" to allow God to do His work on this person and to allow Him to continue to do His work in us. This attitude of faith relieves us from being judgemental.

Anger is a major problem for many people. It is the unhealthy expression of anger toward others that causes damage. We all want to express it responsibly but that is not usually the way it comes out! The greatest suggestion is to abstain from expressing it to anybody until you have talked to the Lord regarding it for an considerable amount of time!

Expressing revenge only hurts us. The majority of the time our anger gets the best of us. Knowing what we know, and having the relationship with God that we do, you would have thought we would have outgrown it by now. Lord, please help us today to let go of all our reservations that somehow the use of anger is going to further any personal cause.

The abrupt interruption of anger is a reminder that we still have "selfishness" and that it is much stronger than we think it is. It's not a matter of abstaining from expressing it. It is a matter of our relationship with God. It is very difficult sometimes to hand the matter of injustice over the Lord. The solution to our selfishness and anger problem lies way before any "antecedent event".

Self control" is a "fruit of the Spirit" not a fruit of our own efforts. If we lose control we should have never had it to begin with. You see, we are dead in Christ and are to remain so by faith. We are also alive in Christ. The key words are "in

Christ". We don't have God on demand to help perfect our own self efforts to right injustice when somebody offends us. Our life is hidden with Christ in God.

Romans 15:4-6 "WE WHO are strong [in our convictions and of robust faith] ought to bear with the failings and the frailties and the tender scruples of the weak; [we ought to help carry the doubts and qualms of others] and not to please ourselves. Let each one of us make it a practice to please (make happy) his neighbor for his good and for his true welfare, to edify him [to strengthen him and build him up spiritually]. For Christ did not please Himself [gave no thought to His own interests]; but, as it is written, the reproaches and abuses of those who reproached and abused you fell on Me. For whatever was thus written in former days was written for our instruction, that by [our steadfast and patient] endurance and the encouragement [drawn] from the Scriptures we might hold fast to and cherish hope. Now may the God Who gives the power of patient endurance (steadfastness) and Who supplies encouragement, grant you to live in such mutual harmony and such full sympathy with one another, in accord with Christ Jesus, That together you may [unanimously] with united hearts and one voice, praise and glorify the God and Father of our Lord Jesus Christ (the Messiah)."

Journal

DAY TWENTY SEVEN

Sharing in Christian groups

Have you ever noticed that Paul said "I am crucified with Christ" not "I was crucified with Christ"? He wasn't even there when Christ died on the cross. It's because the action that took place at the cross transcends time into the now. All of our sins past, present and future lay on that cross. This is one of the greatest confessions Paul ever made regarding himself and it may be ours!

We need to explain with some intelligence and clarity that the work that was done at the cross has made us new people spiritually. Although we at many times may experience some psychological and social challenges, that never changes who we are in Christ. We explain this in our Christian groups or gatherings. We share that we are anchored in Christ. This information will help our group to be anchored as well.

We share in ways that build ourselves up as well as others. Our groups are opportunities to be encouraged and to be encouraging! We are moving from a state of selfishness into a submission to God and His love for those that He has put into our lives. The arrogance of our ways has been destroyed at the cross but we must accept by faith what was done there.

God has expressed and continues to express His love for us and for others through the opportunity of regeneration in our experience. God is already way ahead of us on this point and sees us all as saints. So we are urged to esteem others as better than ourselves and we can do so because of the gift that God has given to them. Becoming aware of our inconsideration of these facts is a large part of our growth.

1 Corinthians 12:1-4 "NOW ABOUT the spiritual gifts (the special endowments of supernatural energy), brethren, I do not want you to be misinformed. You know that when you were heathen, you were led off after idols that could not speak [habitually] as impulse directed and whenever the occasion might arise. Therefore I want you to understand that no one speaking under the power and influence of the [Holy] Spirit of God can [ever] say, Jesus be cursed! And no one can [really] say, Jesus is [my] Lord, except by and under the power and influence of the Holy Spirit. Now there are distinctive varieties and distributions of endowments (gifts, extraordinary powers distinguishing certain Christians, due to the power of divine grace operating in their souls by the Holy Spirit) and they vary, but the [Holy] Spirit remains the same."

Journal

DAY TWENTY EIGHT

A Christian inventory will reveal Christ within

What are we looking for in our personal inventory? If we are focused on the wrong things we can disregard the most important things about ourselves. We need to take on a Godly perspective of ourselves during this important "inventory process". When we do we will find "Goods" we never knew we had. Our mind will be spiritually altered as we consider in our inventory the power of the blood of Christ that we possess. The blood of Christ is a continuing purifying force and is maintained experientially by our measure of faith. This fact stands alone as the purifying act and drives us into dependence on the Lord, away from our own personal works, and pride.

As we consider the facts an inventory of ourselves will penetrate our thoughts. We stock up on knowledge and we see what Christ has done to make us new. In our fact-finding inventory let us consider the following truths which are in us that are of most value. The truth is we died with Christ. We were buried with Christ. We were resurrected with Christ. We were ascended with Christ and we are seated with Christ above all powers. We possess within us the capacity to trust God for His power in our lives. We must comprehend these facts about ourselves.

Christ has done a complete work within us. We see that our faith in God will produce Christian morals. These morals are characteristics of the Holy Spirit. We just need to know where to look. We don't just look at the items in this inventory. We examine the working parts on the inside of these items. We also find that we are subjected to the spiritual realities that we have found. We find out that we are governed by these spiritual realities. We see that we live under the law of freedom in Christ.

We see that we have within us the capacity to choose and believe. We see that we have a will that is capable of making a choice. We can know God! God will direct our mind to fully understand what He wants us to understand. When we inventory we need to see ourselves as God sees us! We need to be cautious of any man that tries to lead us through an inventory process that uses the psychological tools of today. It is satan's desire that you have a distorted view of yourself. Keep satan out of your inventory. Satan will shove your face in the dirt and have you digging for worms

Romans 8:31-35 "What then shall we say to [all] this? If God is for us, who [can be] against us? [Who can be our foe, if God is on our side?] He who did not withhold or spare [even] His own Son but gave Him up for us all, will He not also with Him freely and graciously give us all [other] things? Who shall bring any charge against God's elect [when it is] God Who justifies [that is, Who puts us in right relation to Himself? Who shall come forward and accuse or impeach those whom God has chosen? Will God, Who acquits us?] Who is there to condemn [us]? Will Christ Jesus (the Messiah), Who died, or rather Who was raised from the dead, Who is at the right hand of God actually pleading as He intercedes for us? Who shall ever separate us from Christ's love? Shall suffering and affliction and tribulation? Or calamity and distress? Or persecution or hunger or destitution or peril or sword?"

Journal

DAY TWENTY NINE

Still living by morals?

Make no mistake about it. To live by morals alone is to live under the influence of your own efforts. To live by morals at the exclusion of faith does not please God and is not of God.

The words "Go for it and do the right thing" may not be our own!

Our so called "moral" and "immoral" conduct prior to living in the Spirit has been fully worldly and motivated by selfishness. We were not just trying to get our needs met we were influenced by evil. Look at what the apostle Paul said in Romans Chapter 7 verses 18 and 19. He states that in His flesh dwells no good thing. This can be a realistic inventory of us. But now we can inventory the remedy that God has placed within us when we were born again. It has nothing to do with morality. It has to do with freedom from sin.

This purity was established in us as described through our baptism into Christ's death and resurrection in Romans Chapter 6. Romans Chapter 6 gives us the "way" of change. Morals that are genuine flow from this baptism into Christ and are produced by the Holy Spirit in our lives. Can you see the difference between self generated morals and morals that are produced by the Spirit?

To live by morals alone can cause one to be grandiose, self righteous, judgmental, and to have pretence of holiness. Living by this code can cause one to manipulate God's word to fit ones personal purpose, promotion and program of works. It is an incorrect division of Gods word. In the end it will backfire and cause glaring hypocrisy because it is not how God designed one to live!

All of our needs and being come from the Lord directly and has nothing to do with self reliance at all. That is the best kept secret from the church today! Living in dependence on the Lord will not reveal in ones life any immoral behavior. Rest assured. Proper faith equates to proper works

Romans 7: 17-19 "However, it is no longer I who do the deed, but the sin [principle] which is at home in me and has possession of me. For I know that nothing good dwells within me, that is, in my flesh. I can will what is right, but I cannot perform it. [I have the intention and urge to do what is right, but no power to carry it out.] For I fail to practice the good deeds I desire to do, but the evil deeds that I do not desire to do are what I am [ever] doing"

Journal

DAY THIRTY

Self focus does not produce sanctification

Sanctification is living a life of holiness and love through the Spirit by the work that was done for us at the cross. To be sanctified experientially we needed to place our trust in Christ and His expressed love toward us. We also had to learn to place our faith in the finished work of Christ for us and in nothing else as the "way" to sanctify. We can know that we are new creations and we were seated with Christ above all powers. We no longer have to look very long in the mirror at our sins. It's wasn't about our "blemishes". It was about how successful His death was at putting sin away. We didn't deny this reality. We did not dare to deny Christ!

We are honest about our condition and we sat our sight on how God saw us. We were freed from sin! Finally the fruit of the Spirit began to manifest in our lives. Satan attempted to deceive us into self focus in as many ways as He could. Sometimes his suggestions sounded good. They were directed to the pride of the flesh and to personal works. But we knew better. What good were we if we couldn't see the truth that the Holy Spirit was showing us? How we were to re-receive the true power of God if we are running on self focus? Our only solution is to turn to the resurrection and the life!

If we can not admit to our own selfishness what good are we? Selfishness is what we take to the cross daily. It was only defeated and buried by Christ's death. When Christ was crucified God showed His mercy and grace toward us. Through Him we were raised into new life. Christ's shed blood cleansed us of sins past and his body crucified deadened us to any future sins. So we concluded that spending endless hours in self reflection was a sin. It disallowed Christ into our lives. It made us and our efforts the point of contact in our lives. Pride was only dissolved at the cross.

It was no longer all about us. Christ has already defeated the darkness in our lives. Bearing the death of Jesus Christ in our body is what put an end to our character defects and sin. His death manifested in the removal of our sins. We remembered that Jesus stated that to be His disciple we would have to "Drink His blood and eat His flesh". We know that many of His followers left Him at that time. They couldn't wrap their mind around the meaning of those words. We didn't want to be like those who left Him. Are you one of them? If not be leery of any advise that is given to you that doesn't include the facts of God's grace given to us through His cross.

John 6:53-56 "And Jesus said to them, I assure you, most solemnly I tell you, you cannot have any life in you unless you eat the flesh of the Son of Man and drink His blood [unless you appropriate His life and the saving merit of His blood]. He who feeds on My flesh and drinks My blood has (possesses now) eternal life, and I will raise him up [from the dead] on the last day. For My flesh is true and genuine food, and My blood is true and genuine drink. He who feeds on My flesh and drinks My blood dwells continually in Me, and I [in like manner dwell continually] in him."

Journal

DAY THIRTY ONE

My toolbox of broken tools

My Christian life is one that involves victories and occasional defeats experientially. This corrupt body of mine seems to find its opportunity to express itself in the most frustrating situations. Knowing what I know I still have my moments of anger. Doing nothing and trusting in the Lord seems to be one of my greatest challenges. I've read books on temperament all to no avail. I've been to counseling sessions and assertiveness training courses and the problem remains. I have been given the "tools". Eventually all these tools failed and my so called toolbox was filled with broken tools.

Broken wrenches, screwdrivers, and hammers! I can not be programmed by me.

When I first came into recovery I needed the help of a recovery group. I would sit in the back of the room. I noticed that the call to "come to believe" and the call to "make a decision" was there. It seemed to be to ambiguously stated. However, those may have been the most important words I was ever called to consider. It was very important to me that I got "right" what to believe and what type of decision I was going to make. Believing in Christ and deciding to take advantage of the freedom He won for me at the cross made all the difference in the world. A focus on God's plan of redemption through His blood for me was crucial.

All that I have is a belief that God will somehow do for me what I can not do for myself. The most used tool in my tool box was the will. It caused more damage than any other tool. The will is a strange thing. We can't live by it alone. That's why God works in us both to will and to do. The best thing we can do with our will is make a decision to surrender it to the lord. It is then we are overtaken by our choice. We will experience "I can do all things through Christ" or we will experience the consequences of making a bad choice. The choice is ours. God or Satan. Our best choice is to believe in and choose to trust in the finished work of Christ.

Because of His finished work we are completely set free from bondage to sin and are now placed above all powers and principalities. We use our will to make the choice to place our faith in Christ and Him crucified. It is then that we grow to understand the resurrected life! Our will initiates our faith to believe in whom Christ is and in the work that He has done for us at the cross. We are already changed in God's sight. In God's eyes we are made new and complete. The old man we were ended at Christ's finished work. Our decision and belief is based on the case that was settled and paid for by Christ.

Galatians 3:2-3 "Let me ask you this one question: Did you receive the [Holy] Spirit as the result of obeying the Law and doing its works, or was it by hearing [the message of the Gospel] and believing [it]? [Was it from observing a law of rituals or from a message of faith?] Are you so foolish and so senseless and so silly? Having begun [your new life spiritually] with the [Holy] Spirit, are you now reaching perfection [by dependence] on the flesh?"

Journal

DAY THIRTY TWO

An inventory of what?

In regards to doing a personal moral inventory the buyer must beware! Be leery of those who guide you by the hand in this endeavor. What are they trying to show you? Doing a personal inventory should raise concerns for the person in recovery. However, an inventory can be simply a listing of positive and negative moral behaviors. It can also include a detailed description of these personal traits. A detailed description will include the inward working of right and wrong conduct. The measuring stick should be Christ crucified.

Is this conduct coming through Christ's finished work at the cross or is it generated by the self? Any way you look at it an inventory should always draw us closer to dependence upon Christ's shed blood. Yes, we have hurt people but if we don't get right with God we will continue to do so. And there is so much more for the Christian than doing a moral inventory. We have Christ within and Christ shouldn't be overlooked at the expense of self reflection and the time it takes to detail all the wrongs and rights that we have committed. Although we should take responsibility for our lack of faith this does not include allowing satan to shove our face in the dirt of our past. The blood of Christ is sufficient to remove sins.

When we do our inventory it helps us to recognize our most valuable asset. It helps to recognize that we are new creations in Christ. It is also important not to get side tracked. This will require of us an understanding that it is not an analysis alone that brings change. The changes that we need in our lives have already been made by Christ's finished work! At the cross and the tomb we were recreated in Christ. We were crucified and resurrected with Him. This must always be the focus of a personal inventory. We were meant to acknowledge these truths in our self examination.

The Lord will reveal truths to us that will confirm what it means to be His child. As we look within we also see that God resides in our hearts and that we have the faith that is needed to live this life. We see that we have God's potential. We see that God's will and His love can take ascendancy over our lives. We see that our needs and our calling are under God's providence. We see that the Holy Spirit has given us a mission to be carried out with His power. We see that the Holy Spirit has the ability to do for us what we can not do for ourselves! Try an inventory of Christ within and all His benefits

1 Corinthians 11:31-32 "For if we searchingly examined ourselves [detecting our shortcomings and recognizing our own condition], we should not be judged and penalty decreed [by the divine judgment]. But when we [fall short and] are judged by the Lord, we are disciplined and chastened, so that we may not [finally] be condemned [to eternal punishment along] with the world."

Journal

DAY THIRTY THREE

This is our reality

Sometimes we neglect to see what was accomplished at Christ's cross when the importance and value of that cross needs to penetrate into the most difficult areas of our lives. We get caught up into thinking that it is about "us" and our ability to "cope". That is just worldly psychology. It's really not about us and our progress. The reality is that it's about the perfection of Christ's redeeming work at the cross. Our illusion of being independent is what keeps us wrapped up in ourselves and under the power of the enemy.

Complete dependence on the power of the blood of Christ is the only thing that can set us free. Through the study of the Apostle Paul's epistles we are shown specifically that all our sins have been taken from us. We are also shown that now we are children of God! We are and we become perfect in Him all at the same time. When we are yielded to His finished work we move from glory to glory. However our focus needs to be on Him.

Christ has made us a new creation. This is our reality. But if we doubt Christ and His finished work at the cross we lose this experience and our focus goes back on ourselves. The truth is that all of our sins were placed on that cross. When we fully trust in the work of Christ's shed blood we will experience for ourselves the removal of our sinful character defects and imperfections. A funny thing about this grand effort of ours to improve ourselves was that we crazily thought that we were doing God a favor. But in order to make a success out of our personality we had to line ourselves up through faith in how God operates.

God gives us a sufficient perspective on the problem of sin. Then we had to learn that in Christ all our sins were eliminated. We also learned from the Apostle Paul in Romans chapter 7 that any attempt to improve ourselves would only make things worse. Modern psychology teaches us to place spiritual thoughts into our mind and that will give us the success we need. This is false teaching. The truth is that we use our "mind" to learn of the spiritual and then our "will" to choose to accept by faith the finished work of Christ. Can you see the difference between the two?

James 4:4-6 "You [are like] unfaithful wives [having illicit love affairs with the world and breaking your marriage vow to God]! Do you not know that being the world's friend is being God's enemy? So whoever chooses to be a friend of the world takes his stand as an enemy of God. Or do you suppose that the Scripture is speaking to no purpose that says, The Spirit Whom He has caused to dwell in us yearns over us and He yearns for the Spirit [to be welcome] with a jealous love? But He gives us more and more grace (power of the Holy Spirit, to meet this evil tendency and all others fully). That is why He says, God sets Himself against the proud and haughty, but gives grace [continually] to the lowly (those who are humble enough to receive it)."

Journal

DAY THIRTY FOUR

The Christians experience, strength, and hope

Our faith is not in ourselves but in what Christ has done for us. He put to death the old man we were. He broke the power of the flesh and its ability to hold us. He made us new. Wow! It all happened at the cross when He shed His blood. It is when we come to an understanding of the spiritual that we share our experience with others. We share it in a way that others can easily understand it. This may require us to break it down to its simplest form.

We share that we found the problem to be sin and the solution to be Christ crucified and resurrected for us. We share that we have found power in the meaning of His shed blood. This may sound foreign to some in our group and they may wonder why we put so much emphasis on this point. That is because it goes against the thinking that people can handle their problems on their own. We don't just come to groups to hear ourselves talk. We come to group to hear of our solution in the Lord and to glorify the Lord.

We share our experience, strength, and hope with other people. We also come to group to listen to the experience, strength, and hope that other people share. We come to group to learn of Gods word. We all come together to support one another in the faith. Church is when people come together, support one another and praise God! That's what we do in our groups.

Our personal neediness removes all arrogance. We are all equally needy. We all equally need the Lord so we plead the same purifying blood we so desperately need for ourselves for others as well. When we honor the work that was done at the cross we can see ourselves and other Christians as God sees us. We can see ourselves as baptized into Christ's death, burial, and resurrection. Let us all trust that the Lord has met all our needs!

Romans 3:3-5 "What if some did not believe and were without faith? Does their lack of faith and their faithlessness nullify and make ineffective and void the faithfulness of God and His fidelity [to His Word]? By no means! Let God be found true though every human being is false and a liar, as it is written, That you may be justified and shown to be upright in what You say, and prevail when you are judged [by sinful men]."

Journal

DAY THIRTY FIVE

The antidote for shortcomings

We look at the antidote to our shortcomings which is always found in "God's part" in our lives. He has made us a new creation! Our complete view of ourselves now takes in the reality that we abide fully in Christ. Our perspective is the cross has freed us completely from the bondage to "self". This is because the old man that we were died there. When we observe how God has recreated us we see that He has broken the power of our selfishness and our unbelief. These no longer have to be a part of who we are and what we do.

We see that selfish behavior patterns are simply habits we picked up from the old man we use to be. We can throw this unbelief and bondage to self out! We have a will that can initiate a good choice to believe. The result of committing our belief and choice to the Lord will be the fruit of the Spirit in our lives. This in turn will produce the morals that we are looking for as Christians. It starts with our baptism into Christ's love.

Our baptism into Christ's love and what happened at the cross will translate into our behavior. The basis of our behavior must always be faith in the death, burial and resurrection of Christ. "God's part" is the fact that He made a finished product out of us. When we look at ourselves we look beyond that which is seen with our own eyes and we look into the spiritual. We perceive holiness within ourselves because we see Christ within. We take into account that all of our sins have been removed by the cross.

We are already who we need to be through Christ. Christ has no "character defects" and when He went to the cross to die He took on all our "character defects" and the consequences of our "shortcomings". He not only died for our sins He also died unto them. There is nothing we can do on our own to earn perfection or anything close to it. Perfection is placed in us by God through what Christ did for us. The truth is that at the cross Christ put to death our old sin nature. We need to take stock of Christ's finished work for us.

Romans 5:16-18 "Nor is the free gift at all to be compared to the effect of that one [man's] sin. For the sentence [following the trespass] of one [man] brought condemnation, whereas the free gift [following] many transgressions brings justification (an act of righteousness). For if because of one man's trespass (lapse, offense) death reigned through that one, much more surely will those who receive [God's] overflowing grace (unmerited favor) and the free gift of righteousness [putting them into right standing with Himself] reign as kings in life through the one Man Jesus Christ (the Messiah, the Anointed One). Well then, as one man's trespass [one man's false step and falling away led] to condemnation for all men, so one Man's act of righteous-   ness [leads] to acquittal and right standing with God and life for all men."

Journal

DAY THIRTY SIX

Our confession is that our needs are met

We can not live this Christian life on our own. In order to succeed we need the move of the Spirit in our lives. This was a hard but necessary truth to learn in our regeneration. It propelled us out of Romans Chapter 7 and into Romans Chapter 8. A good confession will include our under-standing that change comes through the cross and Christ's shed blood. This confession will benefit not only ourselves but others who hear us. The finished work of Christ is the simple truth yet it is so hard for people to see. It goes against everything we have learned in which we take pride in.

We have been taught to "get it all" and to apply self effort. And we all have spent an inappropriate amount of time trying to do so. Good insight expresses the fact that when we tried to control our life it only furthered within us grave char-acter defects and shortcomings. Being able to share this distinction is proof that we have an understanding of the gospel. It exhibits growth on our part and the message of Christ crucified and resurrected advances.

The truth that will get us through our struggles is the fact of our baptism, burial, and resurrection with Christ. This can't be overstated! We can confess that we placed all our spiritual, psychological and social needs in the Lord and what He did at the cross. We can confess that we now see ourselves as God sees us. We acknowledge that all our sins have been brought to the light and laid down at Christ's cross. We can own the fact that because of the blood of Christ we are not guilty. We confess that now we can let go of excessive self concern and that now we can start enjoying our life.

We share the fact that having our social needs met isn't what frees us. Having our thoughts in order isn't what frees us. That is the psychosocial. What frees us is the truth and the truth is found in the spiritual. The truth is Jesus Christ. Our confession is we know Him and because we know Him we are free. This confession is easily made to our Christian brothers and sisters. It is with them that we can confess who we are in Christ and share our struggles or sins if we have fallen short. A good inventory of oneself is necessary if one is to share honestly. There are many challenges in this life to discuss. But we do not neglect the work that Christ created within us!

Romans 8:5-7 "For those who are according to the flesh and are controlled by its unholy desires set their minds on and pursue those things which gratify the flesh, but those who are according to the Spirit and are controlled by the desires of the Spirit set their minds on and seek those things which gratify the [Holy] Spirit. Now the mind of the flesh [which is sense and reason without the Holy Spirit] is death [death that comprises all the miseries arising from sin, both here and hereafter]. But the mind of the [Holy] Spirit is life and [soul] peace [both now and forever]. [That is] because the mind of the flesh [with its carnal thoughts and purposes] is hostile to God, for it does not submit itself to God's Law; indeed it cannot.

Journal

DAY THIRTY SEVEN

Keeping complacency out of our groups

Many people come to our gatherings with many kinds of needs. We should adjust our recovery groups or small group's gatherings to meet this persons needs. Sometimes it's not all about the "life" of the group. Even though the life of the group is important, it's more about the life of the person in need. If the newcomer to our group is born again it's just about us hooking this person up to what they already have but have possibly lost touch with. That is an attachment to Christ within. Belief and choice have been destroyed and now is the time to find the Lord and have their faith restored.

Hurting Christians need to become reacquainted with the facts. The facts are that the old person that they were is dead and a new creation exists within them. It is also a time to realize that this is made possible by what Christ has done for them at the cross and all that is needed is an acceptance of the facts. This is the truth that breaks addiction and sin in ones life. It comes through the death, burial and resurrection of Jesus and our attachment to that event.

Through the cross comes not only life but also a way that can be lived by. Again, we were buried and raised with Christ. Pointing this out to the newcomer through our own personal testimonies and talks can make the difference. We as a group must have a single message. The message is that we can not save ourselves. Freedom comes from Christ alone and His method of providing it. Backslidden Christians struggle with addiction and sin because they have forgotten who they are and have made bad choices. So in a very real way we are dealing with complacency.

Complacency is an enemy to the group and to the individuals who attend our groups. We must also guard against complacency within ourselves. We should warn our newcomers as well as ourselves that we need to separate ourselves from the influence of "people, places and things" that are of this world. This is an often times forgotten advice. The influence of non-Christian friends can be detrimental. We survive with other Christians in a hostile world. Let us be prepared to take on the victims.

Psalm 1:1-3 "BLESSED (HAPPY, fortunate, prosperous, and enviable) is the man who walks and lives not in the counsel of the ungodly [following their advice, their plans and purposes], nor stands [submissive and inactive] in the path where sinners walk, nor sits down [to relax and rest] where the scornful [and the mockers] gather. But his delight and desire are in the law of the Lord, and on His law (the precepts, the instructions, the teachings of God) he habitually meditates (ponders and studies) by day and by night. And he shall be like a tree firmly planted [and tended] by the streams of water, ready to bring forth its fruit in its season; its leaf also shall not fade or wither; and everything he does shall prosper [and come to maturity]."

Journal

DAY THIRTY EIGHT

Extending forgiveness

We as human beings have experienced massive relationship problems and it is no surprise that God would teach us many things about human relationships. To a degree we still have a long way to go but God's commandment to love is being followed. We have learned that it only comes through His ability. When we are surrendered God does for us what we can not do for ourselves. Many times in our Christian life demons are on the attack but we attribute our conflicts to human reasoning and interaction instead.

It's not hard for us to get angry when somebody close to us criticizes us hard and in the wrong fashion. More than likely we needed the criticism but if we don't let go of our anger completely we will walk in darkness. The enemy attempts to hold us in bitterness and then the Holy Spirit reminds us about Jesus and all the blessings found in Him. It is much better to be "in Christ". In God's love we can stay the course and loosen up on our bad attitude!

Many of us had our moments of anger that were on the edge of being rage. And many of us have experienced rage in our not so distant past. We have had to get over it. We also learned that if somebody has hurt us and we still talk about it excessively then we obviously carry a strong resentment. We know we have some unforgiveness when we find ourselves talking about another person frequently behind their back. We have all talked about others and have rationized it as well. "I'm just thinking out loud" or, "I need to talk to someone about it" are good rationalizations.

The Bible instructs us against all bitterness. It is evil. Also, if we often bring it up to the person who offended us to inflict guilt, or to maintain control of the relationship, we are not extending the forgiveness of Christ. We need to let the cross and Christ's shed blood reign! Let His forgiveness rule our hearts!

Colossians 3:12-14 "Clothe yourselves therefore, as God's own chosen ones (His own picked representatives), [who are] purified and holy and well-beloved [by God Himself, by putting on behavior marked by] tenderhearted pity and mercy, kind feeling, a lowly opinion of yourselves, gentle ways, [and] patience [which is tireless and long-suffering, and has the power to endure whatever comes, with good temper]. Be gentle and forbearing with one another and, if one has a difference (a grievance or complaint) against another, readily pardoning each other; even as the Lord has [freely] forgiven you, so must you also [forgive]. And above all these [put on] love and enfold yourselves with the bond of perfectness [which binds everything together completely in ideal harmony].

Journal

DAY THIRTY NINE

Our choice and God's care

At the cross the old man we were was put to death. Now our tendency to rely on our own effort has to be put to death experientially. Our own efforts equal our "flesh". Our "flesh" contains within it the memories of what we needed to do to survive BEFORE we were born again and sometimes even after. Our "flesh" remains present in our life and because of its presence we have the capacity to sin. It remembers the "old mans" ways. Our ways as Christians is to keep the "flesh" in check or crucified. The choice that accomplishes this task is to place our faith in the power of Christ's crucifixion.

There are at least two effects resulting from the crucifixion of Christ that took place to consider at this point. One contains the death of the old man we use to be and the other is the broken power of our flesh. To keep the flesh in check we acquire an understanding of what happened at the cross that weakened the power of the flesh. This required a continual study of the effects of the cross and what happened there. We place our faith in the victory that Christ won over ALL powers there. We found that the effects of the cross are inexhaustible and ongoing in our lives. Our faith is what destroys the capacity to sin experientially even though "it is finished" factually.

We are required to take responsibility for the choices we make that result in sin in our lives. The choice that leads to sin is just a symptom of a lack of trust in God's love. It is a rejection of Gods plan for us which is the misuse of choice. When we are in the flesh the Holy Spirit will bring that to our awareness. We in turn discuss our lack of faith with the Lord and lay our efforts down at the cross. We do not over discuss them. We let them die there as they already have through Christ and we submit in obedience to the leading of the Holy Spirit to live this life.

We are required to turn our will and our life over to the action that took place at the cross. What happened at the cross was God's care for us. He doesn't really want our will and our life. He wants us to use our will and our life to make a good choice. He wants us to accept our new life and "will" in Him. It's more of an acceptance of our condition in Christ than a moment to moment choice although it may come to that.

1 Peter 1:2-4 "Who were chosen and foreknown by God the Father and consecrated (sanctified, made holy) by the Spirit to be obedient to Jesus Christ (the Messiah) and to be sprinkled with [His] blood: May grace (spiritual blessing) and peace be given you in increasing abundance [that spiritual peace to be realized in and through Christ, freedom from fears, agitating passions, and moral conflicts]. Praised (honored, blessed) be the God and Father of our Lord Jesus Christ (the Messiah)! By His boundless mercy we have been born again to an ever-living hope through the resurrection of Jesus Christ from the dead, [Born anew] into an inheritance which is beyond the reach of change and decay [imperishable], unsullied and unfading, reserved in heaven for you"

Journal

DAY FORTY

Who we are and what we believe

We would describe ourselves as Christians who have the desire to find Christ in our life and to genuinely love others with the love of God. We would love to do as Jesus did and expose the works of satan and bring our fellow man hope. We would like to know that everything is taken care of by God and that we serve as His representative in home, with friends and at work. We would like to walk in the spirit without a trace of self righteousness. But we can not do all these things without having to depend completely on Christ, His death, and His resurrection as the "means" of living this life on a daily basis.

The circumstances of our life don't have to be any different than they are right now. Jesus didn't have to work out the details of how and when He would get to the cross. The circumstances for this to happen were prearranged. Christ just went about His business doing good and being completely dependent on His father. So it is for us when we are in Gods will. We are no longer under the control of Satan and must not allow Satan to deceive us. Satan doesn't give up just because we are Christians. His first effort is directed at deceiving us and His second effort is directed at destroying us.

Satan weighs down on us and tells us "you haven't changed". We tell Satan "It's over and it's over based on the facts. My sins past, present and future were nailed to Christ's cross. My old lifestyle was nailed to that cross. We tell satan "Whatever sinful situation I have found myself in was nailed to the cross. My shortcomings and character defects were appropriately handled there". The world uses belief to create a better view of themselves. We accept Christs blood, His cross, and His love for us.

Satan would prefer that you make your decision to believe in yourself and continue on in self reliance. However, we believe as a result of the facts that God has established in our lives when He recreating us. We believe the truth and then we trust in the truth by choice. We respond with belief to the new life God has given us. Our belief is a gift of love given to us directly from God. It takes belief on our part to decide to make a stand on Christ's accomplishment

Psalms 103:10-12 "He has not dealt with us after our sins nor rewarded us according to our iniquities. For as the heavens are high above the earth, so great are His mercy and loving-kindness toward those who reverently and worshipfully fear Him. As far as the east is from the west, so far has He removed our transgressions from us."

Journal

DAY FORTY ONE

Self reflection

Most of us have gotten angry, irritated and judgmental in the last 24 hrs. This includes the "mature ones" among us as well. Just because we know the Lord and carry His message it doesn't mean that we are without failure. If we for a moment could step out of denial and be honest with ourselves we may be disappointed and without a doubt the evil one will attempt to bring condemnation. This is what happens when we admit our own non-sense.

But we can't sacrifice self reflection at the cost of a quick solution. Having a restored spiritual experience is contingent on our dependency to trust in the finished work of Christ as our constant solution. This is what is meant by those words "examine yourselves to see if you are of the faith" stated in 2 Corinthians 13:5. As we grow in our experience and understanding of Christ's accomplished work at the cross we will experience glory upon glory. Experiencing the benefits of Christ's shed blood at the cross is the only way to experience peace in our life.

When we trust in the Lord life is good! God gives us all the belief we need and we turn around and place it back in Him and in the way He operates. The event of His death, burial, and resurrection was monumental and gigantorous in its application toward us! Our separation from God is dissolved at the work of the cross only. Our unbelief and fear crumbles when it is taken to the Lord. But the blood of Christ is not to be used like fuel to fill a car up so that it can go. This is reducing the use of the blood into a mechanical equation arranged to a selfish ends. NO! It's more like an eternal energy source that permanently resides in the universe and abides in the heart of the believer. It flows from the heart of God and God is love.

We don't use the blood upon our own personal demand and time either! We speak the blood of Christ not for our life but as our life. We drink this blood. Do you find this offensive or strange? Perhaps you know little about the power of the blood of Christ as it applies to daily living. If so you may be engaged in self effort to live this Christian life. This is known as a "flesh walk". The solution is always found in what Christ did for us at the cross!

2 Corinthians 13:5 "Examine and test and evaluate your own selves to see whether you are holding to your faith and showing the proper fruits of it. Test and prove yourselves [not Christ]. Do you not yourselves realize and know [thoroughly by an ever-increasing experience] that Jesus Christ is in you unless you are [counterfeits] disapproved on trial and rejected?"

Journal

DAY FORTY TWO

Satan's ploy and our character defects

Our change comes through Christ's death, burial, and resurrection. It is the blood of Christ cleanses and purifies our conscious. When sinful "character defects" are found within, it gives us the opportunity to renew our minds. Our mind is renewed by placing it on who Christ is to us, who we are in Christ, and what He will continue to do for us. This is where we join with the mind of Christ. Being joined with Christ's operation of His shed blood will have an impact resulting in the elimination of sinful character defects.

God's strength is made perfect in our weakness. Satan attempts to use fear to push us into self reliant effort. We end up like the Apostle Paul in the 7th chapter of Romans. Doing the thing that we know we shouldn't. As satan taunts us "do what is right, do it, do it" he is attempting to get us to respond to him and act out in self reliance. Self reliant effort that is motivated by deception doesn't work!. This is satans ploy and it leads to failure. This is the scriptural view of character defects and how they originate.

The Apostle Paul stated that "I was alive once without the law, then the law came and I died" What this means is Paul was set free by the new creation of Christ's cross and then satan came to him with the sciptural law. Paul was set free from the law. When Paul acted out in self reliance to do what was right He placed himself back under the law. Satan attempts to do this with us. Our character defects are a symptom that satan has succeeded in his attempt to place us under law and into self reliant effort. The idea of changing our thoughts to "line up with scripture" needs to be properly understood. It could be in error if it keeps us focused on ourselves.

The transformation through the renewing of the mind comes from the everlasting blood of Christ and listening to the Holy Spirit. It's more of a power outside of ourselves working through us. The point of focus is off of ourselves. We don't live according to Christian values we live out of our relationship with the Lord and within the parameters of how the Lord decided to show us His love at the cross. Out of this relationship comes Christian values. We are governed by freedom in Christ Jesus. We wrongly "divide" the word of truth when we make "law" out of Christian principles!

Romans 7:18-21 "For I know that nothing good dwells within me, that is, in my flesh. I can will what is right, but I cannot perform it. [I have the intention and urge to do what is right, but no power to carry it out.] For I fail to practice the good deeds I desire to do, but the evil deeds that I do not desire to do are what I am [ever] doing. Now if I do what I do not desire to do, it is no longer I doing it [it is not myself that acts], but the sin [principle] which dwells within me [fixed and operating in my soul]. So I find it to be a law (rule of action of my being) that when I want to do what is right and good, evil is ever present with me and I am subject to its insistent demands."

Journal_____

_____

_____

_____

_____

_____

_____

DAY FORTY THREE

Turning it over again

God wants us to let go of our own efforts to live this life. So why is there so much teaching given instructing us to apply self effort? Is it because it feeds our pride? I sure hope not. However, people will seek out "self help". "Self help" can only create in us our own efforts. Again, it is God's power that delivers us. We don't improve ourselves. We are set free by God alone. We are rescued from ourselves. Our part is to place our belief in Christ and to make a decision to take the victory over sin that He won for us.

Ultimately, it is not even our belief that activates God's power. Our decision is a response to God's power. So what is the latest "series" or "teaching" topic you are involved in?

We need to beware! A program of personal works cloaked in religious topics may look Holy, but it's not Jesus. True humility is found at the foot of the cross and a clinging to the power of His blood. If you were to mark down how often the word "blood" was mentioned in your self help manuals would your paper remain empty? If the cross and the blood are just side notes in our minds we are still engaging in a program of personal works. Only the strength found in Christ's death, burial, and resurrection can bring completion.

Only the finished work of Christ can remove character defects and give us victory. The truth is priceless and stands the test of time. Christ didn't just die for the sins we've committed in the past. He died toward our sins present and future. The power of His blood endures time. It is required of us to take a stand of faith in what God has done for us so that we can live this life. In Him we can also be dead to sin. We no longer have to sin.

We no longer have to tolerate these shortcomings and character defects of ours. At least to the degree that they dominate us! Take anger as an example. Anger is usually expressed due to the thinking that what another person is doing is unbearable and we need to let them know it so that they will stop. This thinking gets us wrapped up in our own self effort. The Lord bears all things, believes all things, and hopes all things. God believes in the power of His love expressed through the cross to be sufficient for this person that we target with our anger. We actually are harming this person with the hatred of the flesh. Isn't it better to abide in love? It may look passive from a fleshly perspective. However the compassion found in Christ shed blood is where we find strength.

1 Peter 5:6-8 Therefore humble yourselves [demote, lower yourselves in your own estimation] under the mighty hand of God, that in due time He may exalt you, Casting the whole of your care [all your anxieties, all your worries, all your concerns, once and for all] on Him, for He cares for you affectionately and cares about you watchfully. Be well balanced (temperate, sober of mind), be vigilant and cautious at all times; for that enemy of yours, the devil, roams around like a lion roaring [in fierce hunger], seeking someone to seize upon and devour.

Journal

DAY FORTY FOUR

Mental illness

Many of us who have addictions or have suffered from addictions can also have mental disorders. If one has serious biochemical imbalances and has been diagnosed by a psychiatrist with any kind of thought or mood disorder this does not mean this person is being punished by God for having had an addiction. Sometimes these conditions existed before the addiction problem or are a natural consequence of that addiction. It is possible to be a child of God who has a chemical imbalance.

Mental illness is not brought on by a lack of faith. It wouldn't be fair to make such a statement. A psychiatrist can be a gift from God. Let him deal with the physiological by prescribing medication. Medications can be very helpful if one has an authentic mental illness. However, medication should never be substituted for placing ones faith in God. The result of the work of Christ's crucifixion, resurrection, and ascension for us happens experientially in our living as we place our faith in this reality.

Even though Christ's crucifixion happened some 2000 years ago it is a time frame of significant interest to us. It is brought into the present moment of our existence through our faith. We access what happened to us there and the love that was shown to us by God. Now is the time to renew our minds in these truths. The facts of what Christ has done for us by shedding His blood may not be fully beneficial until we understand what happened there and then surrender to those facts.

Some may choose to attend support groups. A support group at its best will bring the truths of Christ crucified to us and the meaning of Christ's shed blood. On the other hand a support group at its worst will not mention the blood of Christ and can falsely indoctrinate us. A program that places our focus on Christ and what He did for us is serving its purpose. Only the finished work of Christ at the cross can restore us to sanity. All the baggage we carry has been taken care of at the cross by the love of God shown there. All the sinful behavior we ever engaged in was handled at the cross. All our guilt and shame has been erased at the cross.

2 Timothy 1:7 "For God did not give us a spirit of timidity (of cowardice, of craven and cringing and fawning fear), but [He has given us a spirit] of power and of love and of calm and well-balanced mind and discipline and self-control."

DAY FORTY FIVE

An inventory of faith

A personal inventory is simply a description of you. I have looked at many recovery guides for doing a personal inventory through the years. They all asked me questions about my upbringing. They asked me questions regarding particular areas I might be facing as a challenge today. I was also asked to list my positive and negative traits. I was often taught to offset my negative traits with positive traits lest my inventory become too gloomy. I was asked to list my harms done to others and rightfully so. However this is not exactly the entirety of how a Christian inventory is to be done according to scripture.

The scripture actually instructs us to closely examine our "faith". When we do a moral inventory we should look at what is behind this morality that we find. If we think that we can do this inventory without greatly considering the changes that occurred for us when Christ gave His body and shed His blood we will be thoroughly deceived. He broke the power of our sins upon His crucifixion. He put to death the old man we use to be.

Our work is to seek an understanding of how God operates. We must see within ourselves an action that was taken outside of ourselves. The action that was taken for us was done by God and that action is Christ and Him crucified. Through an appropriate inventory of self we can examine our faith in this fact. Our faith is what will make the difference. What God does for us is He points out areas in our lives that we fall short of faith in what He has done for us. In a sense it becomes His inventory of us as he shapes and molds us. We in turn take our shortcomings of faith, admit to them and apologize to the Lord. He in turn points us to the finished work of Christ.

Belief, decision, and accountability factor into our inventory. Is it there? Are we making decisions that are lining up into an agreement with God? Are we "letting go" of the process of controlling our own lives? Is there abandonment? Are our lives and decision making turned over to Him? Do we know that it is in Him that we live? All these things are possibilities within you and need to be included in on your inventory. Having faith in Christ will allow you to answer every question with a "yes"!

Psalm 139:23 "Search me [thoroughly], O God, and know my heart! Try me and know my thoughts"

Journal

DAY FORTY SIX

Relationships through Gods love

If you browse your local book store you will find many writings on how to have successful relationships. How many of these publications refer to the blood, death, burial and resurrection of Christ as our solution? As Christians the thought of placing any trust in a "relationship manual" that does not mention the blood of Christ as the solution should be out of the question! A change in perspective in regards to relationships can only come through Gods love and His finished work done for us at His cross.

Setting boundaries can cancel out the work of the Holy Spirit but this may not always be the case. Jesus instructed us to rebuke those who have sinned against us. However, the finished work of Christ needs to be the bases of our love toward others. Our faith in God and what he has done for us to create us anew is what is needed for us to experience a change in our relationships. Our inconsideration of God in our social situations is atheistic. Yet nobody is guided by God all the time and others will offend us and we will offend others at some point. We so desperately need the mercy and grace of God operating in our lives. Does this mean that we excuse ourselves and others from being held accountable? No.

We are all responsible to depend on the Lord to lead us in regards to the relationships we find ourselves in. The healing power of His blood was an act to resolve injuries done on all of humanity and that, of course, includes us! Let our calculations be according to Christ's finished work at Calvary. Celebrate Christ's death, burial and resurrection! Remember that love bears all things, endures all things and believes all things! If others treat us badly and we take an ungodly response it is always our responsibility to take accountability for our response. We can not blame others for our responses.

Our ungodly responses must be taken to the cross. It is our responsibility to trust God to do all He can to deliver us from contempt toward one another. Placing "me" into the equation while neglecting God can only create error. God loves humanity and He sees worth in every individual. We don't always do so. When we don't, apologies are always in order regardless of our excuses for our unloving act. Not only do we need to apologize to the person we may have offended we also need to thank God for His patience with us when we misrepresent Him and fail to yield.

Ephesians 4:31-32 "Let all bitterness and indignation and wrath (passion, rage, bad temper) and resentment (anger, animosity) and quarreling (brawling, clamor, contention) and slander (evil-speaking, abusive or blasphemous language) be banished from you, with all malice (spite, ill will, or baseness of any kind). And become useful and helpful and kind to one another, tenderhearted (compassionate, understanding, loving hearted), forgiving one another [readily and freely], as God in Christ forgave you."

Journal

DAY FORTY SEVEN

There is no shortcoming in the facts

We don't try to change who we are. We accept who God has made us. In Christ we are seated in heavenly places above all powers. We are identified with Christ's ascension and "seating". We are not dominated by sin. The cross and tomb is where all sin ended for us. The ascension of Christ is where sins lost its power over us completely. We just need to take a deep breath and rest in who we are in Christ! We thought we had to become entirely ready to have God remove our character defects. Then we found out He already has. We are joined to Him and there is nothing that can separate us from Him. That joining is not of our making.

He now lives in us and He is perfect. Can Christ be improved upon? Of course not. So we have perfection living in us. Now God tells us to be perfect as He is perfect. This perfection has nothing to do with self improvement brought about by our own efforts. We are made perfect by trusting Him as our source of perfection. The only sin we commit is to cast unbelief upon God's work within us. This unbelief goes against the work of the Holy Spirit in our lives. There is always an escape through believing what Christ did for us at the cross!

Regarding ourselves the truth is that we are not our own. We no longer have personal ownership. We are now slaves to Christ! We have been bought with a price. Bought and immediately changed. We didn't have what it took to change ourselves. We needed a savior. Now we just simply accept what He has done for us. He died. We died. He rose. We rose! This is the eternal reality.

There is no shortcoming in the facts! We can now have dignity and confidence in our lives. God has already placed His judgment in regards to our sinful character defects. Christ took the punishment for our sins so we could be free from any condemnation. Christ put sin to death at the cross through His shed blood so that we can live free from sinful character defects. Now considering our life, there is no reason for misery.

Galatians 5:1 "IN [this] freedom Christ has made us free [and completely liberated us]; stand fast then, and do not be hampered and held ensnared and submit again to a yoke of slavery [which you have once put off]."

Journal_____

_____
_____
_____
_____
_____
_____

DAY FORTY EIGHT

The patience of Christ

All Christians have been freed from condemnation through the blood of Christ. If we have faith in this fact we will be less judgmental of others because we will know that the price of all sin has been paid. We will be more accepting of others knowing that they are acceptable to God. We will cause less damage because we will be accessing the love of God! In fact, not recognizing what Christ has done for us at His cross and resurrection can be very damaging to our relationships. It instantly places us in satan's playground.

Sometimes people will just flat out disappoint us. When we trust someone to do what is right and they fail it can hurt. But we need to get over it and guard against being defensive. This comes by turning this person and situation over to the Lord. What happened at the cross is the solution and it offers a different point of view. His shed blood for us personally assures us that in no way are we better than others. Christ's blood is shed for everyone because we were all equally evil. The offer of being made into a new person is offered to everyone.

God places in us the ability to see beyond the current conflicts of personality to the worth of others in Christ. The blood of Christ can help to resolve our conflicts with others and remove our character defects. It continues to cleanse in the face of ungodly offenses and defenses. If somebody is antagonizing us, we pray for ourselves and for this other person. In the heat of the conflict this can be an easy thing to forget to do.

We do not attempt to correct our relationships on our own. We allow the forgiveness, patience, gentleness and longsuffering of Christ to reign! These relationship issues are a perfect opportunity to bring the Lord in. Everybody has a burden that can be taken to the Lord. Sometimes it's useless for us to argue with people over issues. Instead of advising we can share the Lord through a simple and short prayer asking God to intervene. We can welcome the Lord into our relationship situation by taking our grip off of it!

Colossians 3:12-14 "Clothe yourselves therefore, as God's own chosen ones (His own picked representatives), [who are] purified and holy and well-beloved [by God Himself, by putting on behavior marked by] tenderhearted pity and mercy, kind feeling, a lowly opinion of yourselves, gentle ways, [and] patience [which is tireless and long-suffering, and has the power to endure whatever comes, with good temper]. Be gentle and forbearing with one another and, if one has a difference (a grievance or complaint) against another, readily pardoning each other; even as the Lord has [freely] forgiven you, so must you also [forgive]. And above all these [put on] love and enfold yourselves with the bond of perfectness [which binds everything together completely in ideal harmony]."

Journal

DAY FORTY NINE

Our confession is extreme

What exactly do we share in groups? Personal sharing requires us to share our daily and overall experiences in the Lord. However, we have learned that too much talk about ourselves can take our focus off the lord. So we share how the lord is giving us grace within ourselves, within our families, and within our work place. It helps us and others when we verbalize insights into how the Lord is moving within the particulars of our lives. We need to remember that we are sharing our day to day story.

We are sharing how the Lord helped us and helps us. Our aim is to testify as to how the Lord has changed our lives and continues to minister to us. We can verbalize the great fact that it is not our job to improve our lives. That it is God who meets all our needs! That He can take away all our insecurities and that we don't have to be motivated by fear anymore. We admit that we have been set free from our own independent efforts and the power of satan.

Our confession is extreme. We profess to others that the lord meets all our needs and that we are not in control of meeting our own needs. We share that we have cast all our cares on the Lord because He cares for us. We share that we don't even have to concern ourselves with what action to take next. We affirm that we are "right where we are supposed to be". We declare that where we are tomorrow is completely up to Him.

We confess that we are dead to sin because Christ died to sin for us. We assert that we are no longer under the control of an unrenewed mind because we know the truth. It's a simple message we share. The message is that if we turn our needs over to the Lord because He has met them. All of them! We share that it will require some honesty, some belief and some good decisions on our part to experience God's grace. We share the fact that if we think we can meet our own needs our needs will control us. Let's continue to share what the Lord has done for us in our groups and gatherings

Revelation 12:11 "And they have overcome (conquered) him by means of the blood of the Lamb and by the utterance of their testimony, for they did not love and cling to life even when faced with death [holding their lives cheap till they had to die for their witnessing]."

_____
_____
_____
_____
_____
_____
_____

DAY FIFTY

The Lords prayer and the Beatitudes

Because of what Christ did at the cross the Lords prayer prayed by the disciples was at least partially responded to. His kingdom came because we were lifted up above all powers when Christ was resurrected and His kingdom is within us. His will was done here on earth because all are invited to be saved through what Christ did at the cross and His love is ever present. His sacrificed body on the cross is our daily bread and His shed blood our daily drink. There is now forgiveness for all through what he did at the cross. We are led out of temptation and satan has been defeated through what He did at cross. To Him be all the power and the glory!

The beatitudes were at least partially fulfilled in all of us when he died on the cross. We are blessed by the cross because we are spiritually poor and in need of the work done there. All of our mourning is met by what Christ did at the cross. We are comforted by what Christ did at the cross. By looking at what Christ accomplished at the cross we are made meek. By looking at what Christ accomplished at the cross and accepting that for ourselves we are pure in heart. By looking at what Christ accomplished at the cross we desire to do what He requires because He has given us His will. By looking at what Christ accomplished at the cross we can show mercy and extend peace. HOWEVER by sharing the message of the cross we are persecuted. But it's worth it!

Salvation for this sinful world is the gift. Being made new is the icing on the cake. God's love is the reason we are saved. It is also through His cross that we are changed not by the practicing of spiritual principles per se. It is mostly about His love and His love was expressed through His cross. It was there at that cross that our old man was put to death and a new man within us was raised. It's through the cross we are saved AND sanctified!

1 Thessalonians 1:8-10 "But everywhere the report has gone forth of your faith in God [of your leaning of your whole personality on Him in complete trust and confidence in His power, wisdom, and goodness]. So we [find that we] never need to tell people anything [further about it].For they themselves volunteer testimony concerning us, telling what an entrance we had among you, and how you turned to God from [your] idols to serve a God Who is alive and true and genuine, And [how you] look forward to and await the coming of His Son from heaven, Whom He raised from the dead--Jesus, Who personally rescues and delivers us out of and from the wrath [bringing punishment] which is coming [upon the impenitent] and draws us to Himself [investing us with all the privileges and rewards of the new life in Christ, the Messiah]."

Journal

DAY FIFTY ONE

Compassion

When we operate in the power of our own efforts to love we will find ourselves running short on compassion. Our own efforts many times carry with them our own self interests, right? I mean nobody wants to be a bad guy. However, compassion that is based in our own self interest has a very short fuse. Compassion can not be given by us alone but when we are in Christ it can.

Compassion requires longsuffering and that is a fruit of the Holy Spirit. We just don't have the patience to be caring and compassionate on our own for any length of time. It's only when the peace of God rules our hearts that God's compassion can be extended. And Gods compassion goes way beyond meeting others basic needs toward placing the highest imaginable value on the person He has placed into our lives.

"Our Part" is always to take ourselves and others and place them into the hands of God. This gets us out of the way. Then the Lord can start to work at amending our relationships. This does not excuse us or others of our offenses. It places the Lords cleansing work into the midst of us. His work saves us from being judgmental of one another. Being judgmental is an attitude toward others. Judging and warning others can be of the lord, being judgmental is not. One is of self interests and one is of the Spirit.

We can see ourselves and others through the eyes of faith in the blood of Christ. Once we know that we can plead the blood over our lives and have our sins removed experientially we can have faith that God will do the same in others. We have this faith because we let go of others and place them into His hands. Knowing that Christ was crucified for our loved ones will bring a good perspective into our lives for them.

Lamentations 3:21-23 "But this I recall and therefore have I hope and expectation: It is because of the Lord's mercy and loving-kindness that we are not consumed, because His [tender] compassions fail not. They are new every morning; great and abundant is your stability and faithfulness"

Journal

DAY FIFTY TWO

Working what?

The talks I've heard about recovery rarely address in depth the issues of the flesh. Instead they were filled with a lot of personal experiences of failure followed by "have to's" that places the "how to" on the individual to take personal responsibility. When we fail to attach the work of Christ crucified to our "believing" it leaves the burden of the conception of God and what God can do for us on us.

My point is that any suggestion to have a concept of God without including the cross is done in error. Also any suggestion given to rid ourselves of our "sinful character defects" outside of Christ's shed blood, death, burial, and resurrection, leads us away from the COMPLETE work that Christ accomplished at the cross. Therefore our focus must come off of own concepts of God and our sinful character defects and placed on the cross where Christ's blood was shed. Christ's blood purifies and perfects! This leads to good moral behavior that is authentically generated by the fruit of the Spirit. This is how God helps us carry our burdens.

He provides His cross, His strength, His perfection and His love for us to experience. We are bound to have moral behavior. However, we don't live by morals! This morality is the outgrowth of the Christian that comes through the placing of his faith in Christ crucified. We live by the Spirit of life in Christ Jesus. We need to make a clear distinction on the inner workings of morality. Some of our so called "self control" was generated through our own efforts in a legalistic attempt to live for God and were not Godly at all. So when we didn't exercise this "effort" generated "self control" we would experience condemnation.

Then there is the "self control" that is of God's Holy Spirit. This self control is completely different. This self control came to us as we pleaded and took advantage of Christ's blood over our lives. It was established at Christ's cross through His crucifixion and sealed through His resurrection. Let it be understood that cure comes from Christ and His shed blood and not just in Christ alone. It is through the blood that we are perfected and will continue to be perfected. That blood is backed by God's love. It is our responsibility to place our faith in His redemptive work daily. It is our responsibility to stand on the promises that the work of the cross provides us.

Hebrews 10:19-22 "Therefore, brethren, since we have full freedom and confidence to enter into the [Holy of] Holies [by the power and virtue] in the blood of Jesus, By this fresh (new) and living way which He initiated and dedicated and opened for us through the separating curtain (veil of the Holy of Holies), that is, through His flesh, And since we have [such] a great and wonderful and noble Priest [Who rules] over the house of God, Let us all come forward and draw near with true (honest and sincere) hearts in unqualified assurance and absolute conviction engendered by faith (by that leaning of the entire human personality on God in absolute trust and confidence in His power, wisdom, and goodness), having our hearts sprinkled and purified from a guilty (evil) conscience and our bodies cleansed with pure water."

Journal

DAY FIFTY THREE

Christ in our relationships

We need the truth about what happened at the cross in regards to our relationships. Relationships can become real crazy and real fast. We can take our right to be wrong and say the cruelest things. We can easily act out in stupidity. There are many books written about how to survive in our relationships. These "how to" books are dangerous. Why? We need a savior not an instruction book or seminar. False teaching neglects the work of the cross and points one toward self effort.

The power is in the shed blood where all sin present and future is washed away. Relationships are tough and require tough answers. But we need to remember and beware for there are many false "ways" and man created instructions that go around and exclude the cross. It is only when we understand that we don't have the capability on our own to forgive that our dependence goes to our baptism and resurrection in Christ. Because Christ was crucified for our sins we understand forgiveness. Now we can understand His forgiveness toward others as well. So we allow His Spirit to love through us.

The truth is Christ's love can flow through us and it can only do this because of His shed blood. It is more than just us changing our habits and the way we deal with others. If changing habits could save us then Jesus wouldn't have had to die on a cross. The blood of Christ alone removes our selfishness. It is about us intimately knowing God's love and being anchored in His love toward others. Rejecting Christ into our relationships is a sin.

To accept Christ into our relationships the blood of Christ must be spoken and pave the way. As long as we live we will have problems with others because people differ in their development. If sin is committed we can always call on Christ for forgiveness! Claiming the benefits of Christ's finished work in our lives moves us beyond ourselves into genuine concern for others. The blood of Christ flows outward. We receive the benefits but it is a means to an end. The end is a tough love in a really rough world.

Romans 12: 9-11 "[Let your] love be sincere (a real thing); hate what is evil [loathe all ungodliness, turn in horror from wickedness], but hold fast to that which is good. Love one another with brotherly affection [as members of one family], giving precedence and showing honor to one another. Never lag in zeal and in earnest endeavor; be aglow and burning with the Spirit serving the Lord."

Journal

DAY FIFTY FOUR

Our message is powerful

By speaking of the blood of Christ as the only solution to our problems we learn how to grow in Christ. When we plead the blood we also seek to understand its power. We also learn not to lean on your own efforts. It is through Christ crucified that we have changed and can change. The deeper our appreciation for Christ's finished work the greater our influence will be in this world. When we carry a message our focus is to please God by carrying the message He gave us.

Many times we will hear people complain "We already understand the blood of Christ, the finished work of Christ, and the message of the cross, move on". However, God has not given us any other message to carry. The message of the cross for us is inexhaustible! When do people get tired of glorying in the cross? Why? Why do people get tired of hearing the message of the risen Christ? It is in Christ's death, burial and resurrection that we have our life!

The world is not interested in the things that we are interested in and some of our brothers have been greatly influenced by the world. Their minds are still in survival mode instead of in trusting God. This is pride and bondage. We plant the seeds of deliverance! If we try to please the man who is in bondage we are not doing him a favor. On the other hand, God is the only one that can change this person's heart and we must guard ourselves from judging the person.

God wants us to treat others with kindness and love. This does not mean that we condone their lifestyle if they refuse to change. This is the message we carry "There are things that the blood took away and there are things that the blood gives." The blood washed away the old man we use to be and draws us into the family of God. Our message can be powerful and effective in the sense that it carries a message of deliverance!

Romans 13:8-9 "Keep out of debt and owe no man anything, except to love one another; for he who loves his neighbor [who practices loving others] has fulfilled the Law [relating to one's fellowmen, meeting all its requirements]. The commandments, You shall not commit adultery, You shall not kill, You shall not steal, You shall not covet (have an evil desire), and any other commandment, are summed up in the single command, You shall love your neighbor as [you do] yourself."

Journal

DAY FIFTY FIVE

Love bears all things

The root cause of all our sins is rejecting Christ and the reconciliation work done for us at the cross. Sometimes satan will use the attack of others in an attempt to get us out of God's will. His goal is to get us to retaliate. When we do he has got us right where he wants us. This evil is more than we can bear on our own. We need the power of Christ's death toward sin to come against the devil. We will need to trust Christ's victory for our relationships.

To make a relationship amends with others we find forgiveness in the cross of Christ and then we let the resurrected life of Christ live in us toward others. This does not release us or others from some accountability. We are all responsible to take our burden of sin to the cross and receive the finished work of Christ. All obligations owed due to emotional injuries were taken care of at the cross. It is through the power of Christ's finished work that we are able to forgive.

You do all you can do to make up for the damage you have done. However, ALL you can do now is allow Christ to live through you! If we find ourselves inadvertently judging, belittling others, or bitter, we will find self effort to be an ineffective means to stop what we are doing. What we can do is go to the Lord over our behavior. By taking it to the Lord we can avoid the trap of attempting to improve ourselves.

We need to trust the Lord to work in our lives. In this way we have His life not ours. All Christians feel sorrow when they carry on in ways that are hurtful to others. We all have our moments of failure. Many times we use denial to protect ourselves from seeing our failures. The cross allows us to face our failures head on and find a resolution. We all need this love that Christ provided us. This love opens up the power to bear all things, believe all things, and hope for all things. This love is Christ!

1 Corinthians 12:23-26 "And those [parts] of the body which we consider rather ignoble are [the very parts] which we invest with additional honor, and our unseemly parts and those unsuitable for exposure are treated with seemliness (modesty and decorum), which our more presentable parts do not require. But God has so adjusted (mingled, harmonized, and subtly proportioned the parts of) the whole body, giving the greater honor and richer endowment to the inferior parts which lack [apparent importance], So that there should be no division or discord or lack of adaptation [of the parts of the body to each other], but the members all alike should have a mutual interest in and care for one another. And if one member suffers, all the parts [share] the suffering; if one member is honored, all the members [share in] the enjoyment of it."

Journal

DAY FIFTY SIX

Peace with others

All human beings are guilty of rebellion to some degree. The difference between us as Christians is that God has made provision for this and rebellion doesn't dominate our lives. What should dominate our lives is the love and compassion of Christ. God has every Human being in His hands. Some accept Him and some don't.

Even with a new mind and heart we must still remain dependent upon the cross to keep our flesh in obedience. When we focus on our brothers or sisters sin more than Christ's love for them we have taken a step away from the cross. All people sin and are disobedient. Again, we need to become aware of the beam in our eye. Only the lord can remove it. This will come about as we trust in the blood of Christ rather in our own ways.

We can experience the self control of the Spirit in regards to our relationships if we stay focused on the benefits of the cross on our relationships. We must choose the ways of love rather than the ways of hate. It's always sad when we carry on in conversation that is not pleasing to the Lord. However, when we lose our focus there is no condemnation coming from God. We are under the law of grace not the law of sin and death.

As we more fully trust the Lord and choose to submit to His word we become easier to approach in our relationships. We are more relaxed by knowing that God is in complete control. We become less irritable and immune to the attacks of satan telling us to defend ourselves. God holds up the standard and that standard involves the working of His cross and the instructions of showing love. Now we can all have peace with God in the midst of our relationships and share this peace with others!

Romans 14:19 "So let us then definitely aim for and eagerly pursue what makes for harmony and for mutual upbuilding (edification and development) of one another."

Journal

DAY FIFTY SEVEN

Completely dependent

There is nothing we can do when we are faced by our sinful character defects. But Christ did plenty. He died for our sins but He also died unto our sin. We place our faith in His work at the cross and abide in Him. As we continuously abide in Him we experience being dead to sin. God has actually placed His nature in us when Christ shed His blood and was resurrected. The old man we were died at the cross and we were released from our former master.

Prior to being saved satan lived in us and we lived in satan. Now we live in Christ and Christ lives in us. This is authenticated by the blood of Christ and can only continue to be authenticated through His blood as a means of living this

Christian life. Not only do we experience the death of ourselves in Christ we also and mostly experience His resurrected life. Prior to our death in Christ all we knew was sin. Now we have new life. We are no longer ruled by self and satan. We are no longer under the delusion that we are an independent person. We are completely dependent on the life of Christ!

God used the incidents of our lives to intervene. Those of us who take the time to examine the ways of the Lord may get a glimpse into this. He did what it took for us so that we could here His message. In order for us to understand God's love toward us we must understand the love that motivated Christ to go to the cross. That love allows us to live the crucified life in regards to our own self effort. God's love allows us to live the resurrected life which produces the fruit of the Spirit. To be entirely ready to have God remove our sinful character defects we must be entirely ready to receive Him as our life in all our situations. His life is perfection!

"Self control" has nothing to do with "self" performing it. Self control is a fruit of the Spirit. Our "self" is not the source of godliness. Self control and godliness come through the Spirit. God has recovered us, is recovering us and will continue to recover us! To be recovered is to regain something that was lost. To be in recovery means we have the power to recover! This is done on a day to day basis depending on our trust in the Lord and in the meaning of His cross

Galatians 5:13-14 "For you, brethren, were [indeed] called to freedom; only [do not let your] freedom be an incentive to your flesh and an opportunity or excuse [for selfishness], but through love you should serve one another. For the whole Law [concerning human relationships] is complied with in the one precept, you shall love your neighbor as [you do] yourself."

Journal

_____

_____

_____

_____

_____

_____

_____

DAY FIFTY EIGHT

Leaders who are crucified with Christ

The success of what happened at the cross of Christ is what allows forgiveness. We don't forgive on our own. We allow God to forgive through us. When we embrace the cross of Christ we are embracing our cross. We can not love others by any other means. The blood of Christ makes peace with God and with one another.

We are more like conduits than containers of Gods love. A container just holds something but a conduit passes something on. What the conduit passes on is not of itself. What is placed into the conduit is what is transferred from one place to another. The conduit is not the source or the decision maker of what is being put into it. It simply receives and delivers. It is in this way that it delivers what is needed by its designer to meet the specific needs it was designed for. It is the same for us. We do forgive and love. However, God is always the source

The problem of attaining personal prestige is the down fall of many of today's Christian leaders. The thought that one is more educated or more important than another is a sin. The thought that one is gifted above others is a sin. The sole purpose of our life as Christians is to share Christ and the fact that He was manifested to take away sin. That is what is important! Not promotion of some devised spiritual success program or promotion of "self".

Christ has done something for us that removes our sins, imperfections, character defects and shortcomings. He died unto all these things and when He rose we rose with Him in newness of life. There is nothing we can do to change ourselves or others! We have been guilty of thinking we are something we are not or that others are something that they are not. We are either "in Christ" or not "in Christ'.

1 Corinthians 4:5-7 "So do not make any hasty or premature judgments before the time when the Lord comes [again], for He will both bring to light the secret things that are [now hidden] in darkness and disclose and expose the [secret] aims (motives and purposes) of hearts. Then every man will receive his [due] commendation from God. Now I have applied all this [about parties and factions] to myself and Apollos for your sakes, brethren, so that from what I have said of us [as illustrations], you may learn [to think of men in accordance with Scripture and] not to go beyond that which is written, that none of you may be puffed up and inflated with pride and boast in favor of one [minister and teacher] against another. For who separates you from the others [as a faction leader]? [Who makes you superior and sets you apart from another, giving you the preeminence?] What have you that was not given to you? If then you received it [from someone], why do you boast as if you had not received [but had gained it by your own efforts]?"

Journal

DAY FIFTY NINE

The Christians antidote for character defects

Character is defined as a person's good quality and traits. A defect is a fault or an imperfection. Character defects are just a different way to say "sin". That must always be in the forefront of our thinking when we talk about character defects. By calling them sin we can easily find the solution to the problem in the cross where Christ died for sin and died unto sin. If we still have character defects, imperfections, and shortcomings it's not God's fault. He offers us an invitation in 1 John 3: 3 " If any man places his hope in Jesus Christ he purifies himself ". Christ is perfect and we abide in Him. If we are Christians then Christ has placed His seed in our hearts and that seed is incorruptible.

Are you ready to accept this fact of perfection and believe it? If not be warned, we have the capacity to choose to align ourselves with the sinful nature that exists in our flesh. If we don't believe in Christ's perfect work within us we will involve ourselves in a self reliant effort to take care of ourselves. This self reliant effort can ultimately lead to our destruction. But let it be understood that we are new creations in Christ and that sin will not have dominion over us. We must make our choices to line up with the power of the blood of Christ. The content of our character equates to the amount of room we give to Christ's cross.

What happened at the cross is the event that unified us with the Lord. That unification happens in our experience when we believe that it is true and accept it into our lives. Because He is perfect and we abide in Him we can be perfect as well. But we must remember that it is His perfection. This is the antidote for character defects and shortcomings! Satan is at work within the children of disobedience. God is at work within the children of obedience. Obedience or lack thereof is contingent on whom you are yielded to.

The sayings that were "only human" are true but it is not to be used as an excuse for ungodly behavior. The blood of Christ perfects us. We love Christ when we follow His commandments but also the required "terms" of following His commandments. His terms are that they are followed by means of His cross in the specific situation you find yourself in. Depressed? Turn to the finished work Christ. Lonely? Turn to the cross of Christ! Communication problems? Turn to the death and resurrection of Christ! Anxious? Turn to the blood of Christ! It is a sweet savor that penetrates into every area of our life. It contains power. It is our solution!

1 John 3:3 "And everyone who has this hope [resting] on Him cleanses (purifies) himself just as He is pure (chaste, undefiled, guiltless)."

Journal_____

_____

_____

_____

_____

_____

_____

DAY SIXTY

The message we are presenting

There are many challenges in carrying the message of restoration in Christ. Many times we refuse to see that we too have major problems. All of us have our limitations and are in need of dependency on Christ. We also live with others who refuse to accept their problems. I would say that the battle is against darkness and demons. But Christ came to destroy darkness and He has done this by shedding His blood at the cross! It's His blood that brings power and light to everything that we are challenged by in this life.

Demons scatter like roaches when the blood of Christ is proclaimed by those who understand what it means and stand in the Lord. However, we also have a mind that has a tendency toward the thought "I've got this". Nothing could be further from the truth. We've got nothing of any value but a plea for the blood of Christ. Anything less is insufficient against the powers of darkness. But sometimes we refuse to acknowledge this. It is infrequently mentioned. If by chance the cross is mentioned it is usually referred to as a historical event only or in the form of a footnote.

This Christian life can not be lived unless one is dependent on what Christ did at the cross. It was there that the old man we were was put to death and a new heart was placed within us. This is the operation of God and any reservation in the way God operates results in a reliance upon "self". Is this the message we are presenting? Is this the message we take to the hurting? If not then what? Is what we are doing related directly to scripture or is it just something we devised on our own or was devised by another man? Are we sharing the new covenant we have in Christ or are we giving into some "how to" instruction manual?

Is the blood of Christ the dominant feature in the messages we are giving or is it hardly mentioned? Does the message being delivered have an emphasis on the love of God and what He has done for us or does it contain things that we need to do on our own? Is there boasting in the Lord and glory given to the work of the cross or is it on a famous name or program in the church? Are we teaching on the finished work of Christ or referring to a success seminar? Are we sharing frequently the power of His death and resurrection or are we incorrectly dividing the word of truth to fit our psychological whims?

Galatians 6:1-3 "BRETHREN, IF any person is overtaken in misconduct or sin of any sort, you who are spiritual [who are responsive to and controlled by the Spirit] should set him right and restore and reinstate him, without any sense of superiority and with all gentleness, keeping an attentive eye on yourself, lest you should be tempted also. Bear (endure, carry) one another's burdens and troublesome moral faults, and in this way fulfill and observe perfectly the law of Christ (the Messiah) and complete what is lacking [in your obedience to it]. For if any person thinks himself to be somebody [too important to condescend to shoulder another's load] when he is nobody [of superiority except in his own estimation], he deceives and deludes and cheats himself."

Journal
_____
_____
_____
_____
_____
_____

DAY SIXTY ONE

He perfects us in our experience.

The Christian is restored to sanity when he is placed in Christ. The new man God created in us is designed to be insulated from sin. Even though we are in the "flesh" we are still righteous. This happens due to the fact that the old man we were was and is crucified with Christ. So now we can only be deceived into insanity by believing something about ourselves that is not true. God requires nothing from us but our belief that he has made us and will continue to make us new men through the cross.

Knowing that God promises that sin will not have dominion over us doesn't allow us to have an unguarded attitude toward sin. We need to examine ourselves regularly. Are we in a state of fear filled self centeredness or in a state of faith? If we are in fear and under the oppression of satan we can call on God now! By faith we can claim the authority of Christ's blood over our life. When we do this our sinful shortcomings will be washed away by His presence. It is only when our faith is anchored in the meaning of His death and resurrection that we will experience "continuance" in the Lord.

Satan attempts to divert our faith. When we lack faith we sin and satan continues to work on us. He is attempting to destroy us. He attempts to impose condemnation. But we need to keep in mind that these impositions are secondary to our lack of faith. Lack of faith in what was accomplished at the cross is our primary problem. We have rejected the power of the cross to change our lives. To have God do for us what we can not do for ourselves we need to cast aside our personal rejection of Christ and the condemnation that satan is attempting to impose on us.

We also need to remind satan that the blood washes away all sin. It is then that we can allow God to do for us what we can not do for ourselves! We need to understand that we will not be perfectly yielded all of the time. There will be many occasions where our faith will fail and the perfection of God will not be expressed. There is one person who did walk in a way that continually expressed the perfection of God and that was Jesus. Now he constantly intercedes for us and that is why we are growing in His image.

Hebrews 5:13-15 "For everyone who continues to feed on milk is obviously inexperienced and unskilled in the doctrine of righteousness (of conformity to the divine will in purpose, thought, and action), for he is a mere infant [not able to talk yet]! But solid food is for full-grown men, for those whose senses and mental faculties are trained by practice to discriminate and distinguish between what is morally good and noble and what is evil and contrary either to divine or human law. "

Journal

DAY SIXTY TWO

Be kindly affectionate toward one another

When we live this Christian life we affect more people than we can imagine. Words and actions spread like fire. So we are instructed in God's word to be kindly affectionate toward one another with brotherly love. We are instructed to owe no man anything but love. We are told that love works no ill will to his neighbor. The Bible states that we are still carnal if we have strife and divisions among us. The Bible states that the fruit of the Spirit is love. The Bible instructs us to be rooted and grounded in love!

Extending the forgiveness of Christ is a problem if we still carry feelings of irritability to the degree that it stops us from sharing the love of God. Not receiving the forgiveness of Christ into our lives creates in us sensitivity toward the self centeredness of others and easily translates their self centeredness into a rejection of us. This rejection will cause us to judge others which in turn cause a sense of self righteousness. Not accepting total forgiveness into our lifestyle can be detrimental toward our relationships. It will give satan a foothold.

When we think about God's will for us regarding relationships certain ideas will come to our mind. We are instructed in God's word to forbear one another in love and to esteem others as better than ourselves. It is also good to remember that we all sway in our walk at times. All of us have a tendency toward a self effort that is independent of God's Spirit. All of us can be deceived. So let's speak the truth in gentleness and with patience.

If anger is expressed "do not let the sun go down on your wrath." If you get angry with others be quick to turn around and make peace with them! The blood of Christ always takes the precedence if we place our faith in the facts of the finished work of Christ. We can claim the healing power of the blood of Christ over our relationships. The solution to difficult relationships is found in what happened at the cross.

Galatians 5:25-26 "If we live by the [Holy] Spirit, let us also walk by the Spirit. [If by the Holy Spirit we have our life in God, let us go forward walking in line, our conduct controlled by the Spirit.] Let us not become vainglorious and self-conceited, competitive and challenging and provoking and irritating to one another, envying and being jealous of one another."

Journal_____

DAY SIXTY THREE

Point others to the finished work of Christ

We as Christians have an obligation not just to share the message of love. We must always share "the way" of attaining this life that we propose. Sharing a message while keeping an invisible cloak over what happened at the cross is wrong. This can set our listener into a personal program of works. We need to point others to the finished work of Christ as the "means" of living this life Christian life. The life others so desperately need is found in the blood of Christ. We need to share the message of the cross and resurrected life as often as we have an opportunity to share!

It's not just from behind the pulpit that this message is shared. The Lord uses us in our small groups, Bible studies, and one on one interaction as well. The Lord is raising us up in a world that has little to no Christian values and has a philosophy that is contrary to the way of God. We must take a stand against the new age mysticism and humanistic psychology that is attacking Christendom and weakening its message. Preaching Christ crucified for our sins and crucified unto our potential to sin is the solution. This is the message that others need to hear.

Carrying a message without a bearing on Christ crucified and resurrected reveals nothing of spiritual value. We are in danger of carrying a false message if we do not preach what happened at the cross, the meaning behind Christ's shed blood, and His resurrection. There is a great need for a simple message. The message is that when Christ died the old person that we were died with Him. His blood purifies us and gives us peace with God. It is only through Christ and Him crucified that we change because Christ also died UNTO sin.

We are also resurrected with Him into new life!! This must be made clear in our "community". We share this message with others because the love of God compels us too. God loves others and sees them as valuable beyond what we can imagine. God wants others to know that He loves people and He has placed us strategically in specific situations with certain individuals so that we can reflect that love. His compassion must dominate and that compassion is found in the eternal workings of what happened at the cross!

Galatians 6:3-4 "For if any person thinks himself to be somebody [too important to condescend to shoulder another's load] when he is nobody [of superiority except in his own estimation], he deceives and deludes and cheats himself. But let every person carefully scrutinize and examine and test his own conduct and his own work. He can then have the personal satisfaction and joy of doing something commendable [in itself alone] without [resorting to] boastful comparison with his neighbor."

Journal

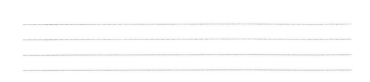

DAY SIXTY FOUR

More of an absolute than a process

It's amazing! Christ can live through us yet we still exist and experience our life. Yes, we make mistakes but we quickly apologize and move on to who we really are. There is no condemnation. We can stand strong in Christ in most of our situations. The blood of Christ cleanses us from all sin! It doesn't have to be a process. It's an absolute! Satan wants to make a process out of it. A long drawn out one.

Living this Christian life requires a greater degree of honesty. Are we resisting the solution that Christ is offering us? Are we being inconsiderate of God's will? This is the sin of rejecting Christ. But we have an option. We can identify and take our weakness to the lord and exchange it for His strength. We can be cleansed by the blood and filled with the Spirit in our life's experience!

We may say "what about self control"? The answer is the fruit of self control can only come from the Spirit as we place our trust in our baptism in Christ. Obedience comes about when we place our faith in Christ crucified and resurrected. This is where the law of the Spirit in Christ Jesus originates and sets us free to be Obedient.

Focusing on ourselves to generate obedience through our own self effort is to make God's commandments "fleshly" laws to follow. We are improperly dividing God's word when it requires much effort to follow His commands. We are not under the law of the flesh! Self effort in regards to spiritual matters always results in failure no matter how successful it appears. It is always ungodly and selfish when we create within ourselves our own personal "law" of self satisfaction and achievement.

Ephesians 4:1-3 "I THEREFORE, the prisoner for the Lord, appeal to and beg you to walk (lead a life) worthy of the [divine] calling to which you have been called [with behavior that is a credit to the summons to God's service, Living as becomes you] with complete lowliness of mind (humility) and meekness (unselfishness, gentleness, mildness), with patience, bearing with one another and making allowances because you love one another. Be eager and strive earnestly to guard and keep the harmony and oneness of [and produced by] the Spirit in the binding power of peace."

Journal

DAY SIXTY FIVE

Church

When many of us started learning the message of grace we started listening very closely to the legalistic messages that we have been presenting to one another. We couldn't understand why we were very rarely hearing any references to Christ's finished work or the cross in much of the messages being shared. Maybe people in general are offended and don't like hearing the word "blood" in our gatherings. Maybe we don't think it is necessary to mention theses things amongst each other. But it is necessary to draw focus on the victory Christ won at the cross.

We know many in our Lords day that didn't like it when He stated to the multitude "You must eat my flesh and drink my blood". Many left His following at that time and He turned and asked His disciples if they were going to leave too. The truth is the message can't be properly presented without bringing a focus on who Christ is and how we have freedom through what He did. We don't want to teach a program of works. Does the Holy Spirit assist us in our own efforts to live this life or does He respond to our faith in what Christ has done for us by shedding His blood and giving his body?

It seems that we have been taught psychological concepts in regards to relationships and now we share psychology amongst ourselves. When it comes to the subject of relationships we are told to do many things to be of service. Some of us seem to have become psychological "one stop shops". We need to avoid the message of legalism and self effort. We need to be careful about using the name of the "Holy Spirit" without mentioning Christ crucified. We should only mention the moving of the Holy Spirit while speaking of the finished work of Christ, His death, His resurrection, the cross or His blood. We must ask ourselves "am I placing the emphasis on Christ crucified when I am giving my friends advice"?

So what can we share when we interact in church? We can confess how we have grown in the Lord and how we learned not to take back what we have given to God. We confess how we turned it over and stayed in a state of trust. We share with our church how we learned to wait on the

Lord to see how He would work out our social and psychological issues. We confess how the Lord worked out our relationships with others and how He improved our personal outlook upon life. Also as part of our confession we can pray the blood of Christ over our lives and the lives of others. These confessions will put the powers of darkness into retreat. Satan needs many reminders of what happened at the cross of Christ. This is an effective way to participate in church

Ephesians 4:24-25 "And put on the new nature (the regenerate self) created in God's image, [Godlike] in true righteousness and holiness. Therefore, rejecting all falsity and being done now with it, let everyone express the truth with his neighbor, for we are all parts of one body and members one of another."

Journal

DAY SIXTY SIX

The Christian message and recovery groups

Groups are simply the assemblage of people together. Groups are not necessarily good or bad. But it is not necessarily a group that we as Christians need. We need a person and a savior. Only Jesus Christ, His cross and resurrection can free us as a people. This truth usually requires a revelation given by the Holy Spirit. Also, there is no freedom found in a group unless it states the truth that is found in Christ!

A preoccupation with a group can replace other addictions but eventually intellectualism must succumb to heart issues. A personal relationship with God the creator will set things straight. A belief in His son plus the knowledge of what Jesus' death and resurrection means to us personally will set us free! It is helpful for us as Christian to make these distinctions.

A restored relationship with Christ is what we want if we find ourselves at a loss due to an addiction. We as Christians are called to live by Christ's death, burial, and resurrection. These "Christian recovery groups" can fill themselves with the processing of personal problems and hardly focus on the absolute truth of Christ crucified and resurrected. We must avoid morbid self reflection. Carrying a message without a bearing on Christ crucified reveals nothing of spiritual value and is in danger of being a false.

Satan's biggest attacks are to get our eyes off Jesus and focused onto our wounds. In our recovery groups we have a passion for those who are bound by drugs and alcohol. Let us share our passion with caring gentleness and without being overbearing. It is the lord Himself that is providing the deliverance that is needed and it comes from His shed blood. He places an unprecedented value on the addict's life. The value is equated to the blood of His dear son.

By sharing who we are in Christ we assist others to stand up in there new status of being raised with Christ above all principalities and powers. We affirm to our group that they can place themselves in a restful state of mind. We also aid the newcomer to place all areas of his life in Christ including his psychological and social concerns. We share that exercising faith in the Lord is not passive and requires action in our trust life. We confess that the guidance of the Holy Spirit must be greatly considered. We confess that we must put our feelings aside and place all our concerns into the Lord's care.

Colossians 3:9-11 "Do not lie to one another, for you have stripped off the old (unregenerate) self with its evil practices, And have clothed yourselves with the new [spiritual self], which is [ever in the process of being] renewed and remolded into [fuller and more perfect knowledge upon] knowledge after the image (the likeness) of Him Who created it."

Journal

_____

_____

_____

_____

_____

_____

DAY SIXTY SEVEN

The Christian who carries the message

All Christians have a desire to carry the message of Christ. This is why the the Lord gives ministry gifts. These ministry gifts are joined with the fruit of the Spirit. It's when we take personal ownership of these gifts that they become misdirected. If we think were hitting a home run when we present in ministry we need to be on guard against arrogance. We didn't come up with the revelation God gave it. So the glory goes to God. We don't create an authentic ministry. If one thinks this is the case, his ministry must be seriously questioned. It can only be planted in the heart of one who is totally surrendered to the work of the cross in his life.

How do you know if you or this other person is truly yielded to God? By your words or the words of this person who claims to have a ministry. Do they line up with the Apostle Paul's "I preach Christ crucified"? Do they teach that a Christian is both dead and alive in Christ? Do they teach that free will is limited to a choice and then we become a slave to that choice? Or are they just delivering a self improvement program in arrogance?

We need to beware of seeking greatness in the ministry that Christ has given us. First off it's not our ministry, its His. Seeking greatness is a ploy of the devil and a temptation of the flesh. The new man in Christ seeks to serve and that new man is owned by Christ. If we feel that we are carrying a message we need to ask ourselves certain questions. When we carry the message are we addressing personal un-manageability and the placing of appropriate belief? Do we address making fitting choices, pertinent self reflection, and to making right our wrongs? Are we presenting the "means" by which to do such things? Are we explaining that it is the "means" that will make a difference? Are these biblical revelations being encouraged to be done through self effort or accepted by faith through the finished work done at the cross of Christ?

Are we sharing that we don't want to attempt to practice Christian ideals through personal technique and effort? Are we explaining that this is what would be called a "flesh walk"? We share the fact that what we want is our actions to be generated by what happened at the cross and to be moved by the Holy Spirit. The problem many times is that we encourage the use of the Bible as a guide book and others misinterpret it and head down the path of self effort. The Bible is a book of revelation of what is bound to take place in the life of the yielded Christian.

Colossians 3:12-14 "Clothe yourselves therefore, as God's own chosen ones (His own picked representatives), [who are] purified and holy and well-beloved [by God Himself, by putting on behavior marked by] tenderhearted pity and mercy, kind feeling, a lowly opinion of yourselves, gentle ways, [and] patience [which is tireless and long-suffering, and has the power to endure whatever comes, with good temper]. Be gentle and forbearing with one another and, if one has a difference (a grievance or complaint) against another, readily pardoning each other; even as the Lord has [freely] forgiven you, so must you also [forgive]. And above all these [put on] love and enfold yourselves with the bond of perfectness [which binds everything together completely in ideal harmony]."

Journal

DAY SIXTY EIGHT

A Christian perspective on "character defects"

I can't tell you how often throughout my life I tried to make a success out of my personality. I didn't like myself. I was impulsive and worldly in many of the things I would say.

This was something I would do often! So this is what I've learned to overcome my "self". Jesus Christ won the victory over sin at the cross. When we abide in Him we have the victory as well.

We have a new resurrected man living inside of us. That new man is dead to sinful character defects and short-comings. That new man was created perfect. He lives in another realm called "The spirit of life in Christ". An over focus on our liabilities is simply created by satan. Our old man and sinful flesh are sealed in Christ's death. Our life is sealed in His resurrection!

When we are weak the temptation is to lean on some kind of personal principle instead upon Christ. But it is in our weakness that God presents a revelation of His strength. As He gives us this revelation we become absorbed in it and He does for us what we can not do on our own. We accept this by believing that God has rewarded us with His grace. His strength comes through the cross and Christ's work done there!

What situation do we find to be a challenge? We can carry the victory and power of Christ's death, burial, and resurrection into that situation. His shed blood is the only solution to that problem. But its HIS cross that becomes ours. Our self does not play into it. The fruit of self control which comes from the Spirit does. The Spirit operates within the statutes which the cross has set up in our lives! Self reliance can not bring the fruit of the Spirit into our lives. The fruit of the Spirit comes about through our faith in the finished work of Christ.

Colossians 3:15-17 "And let the peace (soul harmony which comes) from Christ rule (act as umpire continually) in your hearts [deciding and settling with finality all questions that arise in your minds, in that peaceful state] to which as [members of Christ's] one body you were also called [to live]. And be thankful (appreciative), [giving praise to God always]. Let the word [spoken by] Christ (the Messiah) have its home [in your hearts and minds] and dwell in you in [all its] richness, as you teach and admonish and train one another in all insight and intelligence and wisdom [in spiritual things, and as you sing] psalms and hymns and spiritual songs, making melody to God with [His] grace in your hearts. And whatever you do [no matter what it is] in word or deed, do everything in the name of the Lord Jesus and in [dependence upon] His Person, giving praise to God the Father through Him."

Journal

DAY SIXTY NINE

A relationship inventory

When we start to notice the ungodly ways of those close to us it is very possible that we are blocking out the love of God. Using 1 Corinthians chapter 13 as an inventory tool we can ask ourselves many questions. The first and most important question is "Is the love of God being manifested through me?" If not, we will more than likely answer the following questions with the answer "no". These questions may go as follows; "Is there patience and kindness in my life?" "Is there any gentleness?" "Is there forgiveness?"

"Am I being boastful?" "Is there a bearing of all things?" Etc...

The speck in our brother's eye is not our problem. The problem is the beam in ours. The unbelief in others is simply overcome by them placing their trust in Christ. However, this beam in our eye is not so easily removed. First we have to lay down our pride at the cross where it is removed. We have to admit that we have become the one with the major problem.

When there is irritability in a relationship sometimes it is best to NOT set up boundaries. Of course they are sometimes needed but it can be overdone. After boundaries are sat we start to build walls! This is just more of the "self" taking care of the "self". When boundaries are sat that exclude the move of the Spirit and ones focus on the cross it's most likely of the flesh. Sometimes we need to draw a distinct line between defensiveness and a Godly approach.

When the Lord is using us to work with others we also need to guard ourselves from being disappointed. The Lord may be using us to plant a seed or a message only. But since we are involved we can get so caught up that we can become judgmental. This is because we care but it's not the love of God when we judge. The Lord wants us to understand this!

1 Corinthians 13:4-8 "Love endures long and is patient and kind; love never is envious nor boils over with jealousy, is not boastful or vainglorious, does not display itself haughtily. It is not conceited (arrogant and inflated with pride); it is not rude (unmannerly) and does not act unbecomingly. Love (God's love in us) does not insist on its own rights or its own way, for it is not self-seeking; it is not touchy or fretful or resentful; it takes no account of the evil done to it [it pays no attention to a suffered wrong]. It does not rejoice at injustice and unrighteousness, but rejoices when right and truth prevail. Love bears up under anything and everything that comes is ever ready to believe the best of every person, its hopes are fadeless under all circumstances, and it endures everything [without weakening]. Love never fails [never fades out or becomes obsolete or comes to an end]."

Journal

DAY SEVENTY

Sharing our confession of faith

Our confession before men should be positive and based on the victory that the Lord has won for us. However there will be times of personal struggle when we error and in turn injure others. Being able to confess that we do not trust the Lord in any given situation is the first step needed in order to turn it into trust. This requires us to admit to ourselves that we have been taking the one sided point of view that we are on our own in this life and acting out selfishly.

To rebel and act independent of God is the exact nature of our wrong and always involves others. It means that we are depending on something else. That something is not of God and will cause injury to ourselves and others. When we reach the place in our lives where we understand that what is not of faith is sin we have taken a big step in our understanding.

The exact nature of our wrong includes placing our faith in the wrong source. Proper faith must have an object. To place our faith in vagaries will not do. The point is that we can not separate Christ from His cross

We place our faith precisely in Christ's love and the work that He did for us at the cross. When we are able to share the truth of how we came to understand this fact in our Christian gatherings it solidifies our stand. This also sheds light and healing onto the paths of the newcomer. We know that Christ crucified penetrates into the very moments of our lives. The Apostle Paul stated some years after His conversion "I am crucified with Christ".

Why is it so important to keep this in the forefront of our thinking? The reason is that this is the fact which changes us in our experience. Our old man was put to death on Christ's cross. But there is much more than our death in Christ. Death comes first then Life! We accept Christ's death for us. Then we accept His life. His death and life are combined in regards to how we relate to our lives and the lives of others.

What can we say that will constitute a good confession? We can confess to what Christ has done to set us free. Of course this will require an understanding of what exactly He has done to do so. For starters we can confess that He put to death the old person that we were when we died with Him on the cross. We can also confess that a new man was created in us upon Christ's resurrection. We can confess that this "new man" embedded in us is joined to Christ. We share that if we focused only on our sins and the damage done we would never be able to focus on what Christ can do! By sharing a positive confession we are encouraging our brothers and sisters in the Lord to place their selves in Christ.

1 Thessalonians 3:11-13 "Now may our God and Father Himself and our Lord Jesus Christ (the Messiah) guide our steps to you. And may the Lord make you to increase and excel and overflow in love for one another and for all people, just as we also do for you, so that He may strengthen and confirm and establish your hearts faultlessly pure and unblamable in holiness in the sight of our God and Father, at the coming of our Lord Jesus Christ (the Messiah) with all His saints (the holy and glorified people of God)! Amen, (so be it)!"

Journal

DAY SEVENTY ONE

Improving our conscious contact through the blood of Christ

This Christian life is not about us "feeling good". It's about us connecting with God. When we connect with God we automatically "feel good". But how do we know if we are authentically connecting with God? We can know by the "blood of Christ" and its content in our trust life. Its Christ's shed blood that connects us to God. When we admit our lack of faith in the finished work of Christ, and then turn to the cross, the enemy can no longer place a wedge between us and God. The Holy Spirit Guides us deeper into the meaning of what happened at the cross immediately after our admission of our need for Him and our turning toward Him.

At the cross is where satan's influence on our lives is eradicated. There comes a time when we need to move on from knowing what God can do for us to actually allowing Him to do so in our life's experience. This is when we leap forward in our contact with God. Early on in His move in our lives we won't recognize what He is doing. But the more we allow the Holy Spirit to move in our lives the better acquainted with Him we will be. Christ's work on the cross and His love for us paved a way for this and must remain our object of devotion. If we lose that devotion we lose our experience.

We can know the truth of Christ crucified and resurrected and still sin. Sometimes we will have to experience the full consequences of that sin to let go of selfishness and to know God at a deeper level. Sometimes desperation is just what we need. Sometimes we need something in our lives that will break our stubbornness. This is a sad but true fact! We need to be able to receive what God has for us. God's grace doesn't eliminate standards it raises them to the highest level. It makes available to us the law of the Spirit in Christ Jesus.

We are under a new law now and it still requires obedience on our part. This is the law of freedom in Christ Jesus. The question we must ask ourselves is "is this obedience a fruit of the Spirit or of my own effort?" We can answer this question by asking ourselves another question. "Am I depending on the work that was done at Christ's cross or on me?" There is a vast difference between the two approaches. Is our desire to feel good about ourselves causing us to have a "do-good" addiction, or is the Spirit producing good fruit in our lives and that which connects us to God? If we have a "do good" addiction we are not operating in the law of the freedom in Christ.

1 Thessalonians 5:11-13 "Therefore encourage (admonish, exhort) one another and edify (strengthen and build up) one another, just as you are doing. Now also we beseech you, brethren, get to know those who labor among you [recognize them for what they are, acknowledge and appreciate and respect them all]--your leaders who are over you in the Lord and those who warn and kindly reprove and exhort you. And hold them in very high and most affectionate esteem in [intelligent and sympathetic] appreciation of their work. Be at peace among yourselves."

Journal

DAY SEVENTY TWO

Christ forgives and lives through one another

When we heard that the answers to all our life's problems were given to us at the work of Christ's cross it spoke to our hearts. We had tried so many steps and methods to be good Christians. But the truth is that Christianity is not a method for living that is created within our own efforts. We discovered that our efforts at being good Christians were just causing us problems. When we put forth a personal effort we stumbled. We eventually came to the conclusion that our Christian walk had to be greatly gifted to us by God. This revolutionized our thinking. This especially held true in regards to loving others.

Without being mindful of His shed blood and its meaning we could not love as Christ loved. Being mindful of His shed blood allowed us to stand by in our minds eye and see that Christ was crucified for this person that God has placed in our life. We learned that the Spirit could speak to us in our most difficult times of interactions with others. That was when we were brought into this situation as a carrier of God's love. God's forgiveness and care could flow from our lives as we trusted in Him and the powerful working of His shed blood. Others were extremely valuable and we were commanded by God's word to esteem them above ourselves. This could only come about through our understanding and faith in the meaning of Christ crucified for humanity.

It is not just a sin to judge others. It was a sin to not allow God into our relationships with others. God loves the people He has put into our life and sees the value in them. Christ has shed His blood so that they may be a part of His family. He died on the cross so that we could all stand strong in Him. We do not share His love from our own strength. It is all Him. At our best we just reflect Gods love and it is not self generated. God fed His love into and through our lives as we looked upon Him and the deeper meaning of what it means to eat Christ's flesh and drink His blood. His shed blood cleansed us of our sin of selfishness. Secondly, the death and resurrection of His body made us dead to our selfishness and alive to love.

We have seen that there was a difference between the action of His shed blood and the action of His body dying and resurrecting for us. Knowing and having faith in these truths granted us His ability to love others. As the fruit of the Spirit manifested in our lives and character the "beatitudes" were automatically lived out in our lives too! But to have God do for us what we can not do on our own required us to go through His cross. Our attempts to apply the beatitudes through our own self effort led to heartbreaking failure.

140

Hebrews 3:12-14 "[Therefore beware] brethren, take care, lest there be in any one of you a wicked, unbelieving heart [which refuses to cleave to, trust in, and rely on Him], leading you to turn away and desert or stand aloof from the living God. But instead warn (admonish, urge, and encourage) one another every day, as long as it is called Today, that none of you may be hardened [into settled rebellion] by the deceitfulness of sin [by the fraudulence, the stratagem, the trickery which the delusive glamor of his sin may play on him]. For we have become fellows with Christ (the Messiah) and share in all He has for us, if only we hold our first newborn confidence and original assured expectation [in virtue of which we are believers] firm and unshaken to the end."

Journal

DAY SEVENTY THREE

Excessive self reflection can be a sin.

The scriptures in the Holy Bible explain the fruit of the Spirit and what the Christian life would look like if we were surrendered to God. Every true Christian has prayed to God "Lord please place this fruit into my life for I do not possess it".It was very shortly after that prayer that we became determined to produce this fruit. We thought that through determination we could direct ourselves into production. But this just wasn't happening. So we turned to Christian writers and started reading instructional books. We have read books on "secrets", "steps" and "keys" to live this Christian life. We thought we could learn our way into fruitful living.

To our dismay this learning did not improve our character. This "learning" went on for many years with little results. "Christian" psychology only kept us focused on ourselves. Our sins remained and we were beat. We wanted to rise above our selfishness but we just couldn't. We had a lot more to learn! But what we needed to learn would come to us exclusively from the word of God and particularly from the revelation given to the Apostle Paul which is found in His epistles. All of us had to go through this process to get beyond ourselves.

What we really needed to learn is that sin was put to an end at the cross. We needed to learn the truth that if we are "in Christ" and God has made provision for our sins. The resurrection of Christ also gives us life! "Christian" psychology didn't teach us this. It may have mentioned it as a footnote but then it only put our focus back on ourselves. With the focus back onto ourselves we found ourselves in failure and disillusionment. The more we tried the more we failed. So in desperation we turned to the word of God. Then like the Apostle Paul we received through revelation the message of the finished work of Christ and the message of grace.

It was when we were completely broken that our spiritual eyes began to open up. It was then that we chose to surrender to God's direction. His direction for us is always His cross for us. It was at His cross that our sins were settled. It was at His resurrection that our life was given. But turning our self and situation over to God was an unnatural act for us. To move forward into spiritual obedience always required us to lean back into the power of the blood of Christ. This was the best kept secret and the only real discipline of Christianity. The natural mind didn't understand the dynamics.

There were many ways to walk in error and we had to be forever diligent to check our motives as to whether they were centered on our baptism in Christ. If we didn't check our actions against the cross of Christ we would find ourselves in error. Satan's objective is to destroy us by diverting our faith. Sometimes being redundant with the enemy is all that is needed to get rid of him!

Titus 2:11-12 "For the grace of God (His unmerited favor and blessing) has come forward (appeared) for the deliverance from sin and the eternal salvation for all mankind. It has trained us to reject and renounce all ungodliness (irreligion) and worldly (passionate) desires, to live discreet (temperate, self-controlled), upright, devout (spiritually whole) lives in this present world"

Journal

DAY SEVENTY FOUR

How to love

God's greatest command is for us to love yet the ability to follow this command to love comes through God's grace only. It can not come about through our own self effort and reliance. To follow this command we need to see that Christ is the source of love and then we simply yield to Him. Loving others has little to do with us alone. We stand aside with our self crucified and allow Christ to love thus we follow His command. It is then that we are perfect as He is perfect.

It's never OK to hurt others. If we find ourselves doing so we must stop what we are doing that is hurting others and get right with God. We get right with God by getting out of His way and letting Him love others through us. This requires once again that we take the problem (us) to the cross where we were crucified and resurrected. It is only there that we can see His love and grace for ourselves and for others.

The blood of Christ brings peace with God. But even with knowledge of the cross relationships can be a struggle at times. If we want to punish the people who have disappointed us then it is obvious that we do not possess the forgiveness of God. Now we become the offender because we do not allow Christ into our situation with this other person. We let Christ in by pleading the blood in our current social situation.

Forgiveness comes through the cross and all sins were laid on that cross. We don't produce forgiveness. It comes directly from God. Yes, Christ taught us to pray for forgiveness as we forgive but we couldn't possess that ability until the Holy Spirit was able to reside in our hearts through our baptism into Christ. Christ knew this and gave the promise that He would not leave us alone but would send us the Holy Spirit to dwell within.

James 4:10-12 "Humble yourselves [feeling very insignificant] in the presence of the Lord, and He will exalt you [He will lift you up and make your lives significant]. [My] brethren, do not speak evil about or accuse one another. He that maligns a brother or judges his brother is maligning and criticizing the Law and judging the Law. But if you judge the Law, you are not a practicer of the Law but a censor and judge [of it]. One only is the Lawgiver and Judge who is able to save and to destroy [the one who has the absolute power of life and death]. [But you] who are you that [you presume to] pass judgment on your neighbor?"

Journal

DAY SEVENTY FIVE

It's not "all about us" anymore

When we were saved we knew that something inside of us changed. God was now in our heart. When life's challenges came our way we started to see that we had "old" behavior. So our first inclination was to work on ourselves. That was a mistake that sent us into many wasted years. We attended program after program and read self help book after self help book. What we didn't understand was that we have also been freed of the chore of fixing ourselves.

There comes a point in time when it is time to step away from the "mirror". We can now look to Christ and what He has done for us. We can see that all our faults lay upon His cross and have been forgotten. Our belief in what happened there allows us to experience His finished work. We can not experience His finished work if we are focused on ourselves. It's not even about us. It about Christ! Yet we are "in Christ"!

We don't have to experience living in a selfish state anymore. We have the capacity to choose which type of life we will live. God gives us this gift. This means we have the capacity to live in the Spirit of God or in the ways of sin. Either way comes about by choice. There is no middle ground. We can not operate independently. It's either God or satan. We can either choose faith or unbelief. It's either an acceptance of Christ or a rejection of Christ.

It's surprising to find that we feel more complete as a person living this Christian life. We do not lose ourselves when we are "In Christ". Otherwise the Apostle Paul wouldn't have stated "nevertheless I live". What we lose is our self as the center our life. It use to be "all about us" but that's not Christ!. In Christ we are fully adequate to live this Christian life. The key words are "In Christ". Our inadequacy to live this life is replaced by the power of the blood of Christ and the work of the Spirit.

1 Peter 1:21-23 "Through Him you believe in (adhere to, rely on) God, Who raised Him up from the dead and gave Him honor and glory, so that your faith and hope are [centered and rest] in God. Since by your obedience to the

Truth through the [Holy] Spirit you have purified your hearts for the sincere affection of the brethren, [see that you] love one another fervently from a pure heart. You have been regenerated (born again), not from a mortal origin (seed, sperm), but from one that is immortal by the ever living and lasting Word of God."

Journal

DAY SEVENTY SIX

God's ability

Christ paid a high price for our freedom when His physical body died upon the cross. This was no easy task. At His cross He was putting to death the person we were and creating in us a new heart. Accepting this fact not only changes us but it also has become a means of living for us. Accepting our death and life with Him has become a way of life for us that works. The Holy Spirit beckons us to take advantage of Christ's shed blood at the cross.

There are times we reject Christ into our situations and this is a hard confession to make but when that confession is made it is followed by freedom! At the root of all our sinful character defects is a rejection of God's way for us. It is God's ability as proven by the risen power of Christ that we have complete dominion over our sinful character defects and shortcomings. We will have moments where we fall short of faith but God promises that sin shall not have dominion over us. We are raised in Gods power because Christ died unto sin for us. It is not self generated.

People need the message of the blood of the cross and its meaning. That is the soil in which we grow. This message states that the only discipline that is required of us is faith in Christ and what was accomplished at the cross. The Holy Spirit will take care of all other disciplines in our life! Sin has been dealt with thoroughly when Christ shed His blood. Its only when we believe that God has done for us what we can not do for ourselves regarding sin in our life that we become entirely ready for God to move through us.

Sinful character defects and shortcomings are rooted in our pride. We confess sin and place faith in Christ's finished work to remove them and keep them removed. The best approach is to have the Lord come to aid us. On our own we never become entirely ready for this to happen, it happens and then we say "wow that was God!" His cross and resurrection is our life source.

1 Peter 3:8-9 "Finally, all [of you] should be of one and the same mind (united in spirit), sympathizing [with one another], loving [each other] as brethren [of one household], compassionate and courteous (tenderhearted and humble). Never return evil for evil or insult for insult (scolding, tongue-lashing, berating), but on the contrary blessing [praying for their welfare, happiness, and protection, and truly pitying and loving them]. For know that to this you have been called, that you may yourselves inherit a blessing [from God--that you may obtain a blessing as heirs, bringing welfare and happiness and protection]."

DAY SEVENTY SEVEN

Carrying His message

As ministers of the gospel I believe the Lord would tell us "The message of recovery is the message of the cross. I have given it to you to carry. Present it confidently and humbly knowing that I am the source". We need to keep this in mind as we consider the fact that the scriptures instruct us to "exhort one another daily lest any of us be hardened by the deceitfulness of sin". The scriptures also state to "consider and provoke one another unto love and good works." Of course this can only be done by pointing to our baptism into Christ at the cross which completed a finished work in us.

If we share a message on how to be happy, joyous, and free, we better make sure it includes the cross and what happened there. Claiming the power of the blood is not claimed only for ourselves. It is also the means of giving us power to deliver its message to others. When we are called to service it doesn't mean that we are perfect. It doesn't mean that we possess some kind of special knowledge. And it should not be our intention to govern. Through the grace of God we just find ourselves in a position to be of service.

We who are becoming leaders need to understand that leaders have a greater tendency toward pride. We can't let our message feed our own need for self importance. This flesh of ours wants to be idolized. When God gives us a message to carry we can not take credit for it. The temptation to take too much pride in ourselves becomes strong. The lie that we are more favored than others comes to us. If we buy into this lie, and resort to self importance, the message we carry will not be backed up with spiritual substance. People will disregard us and the message we carry! We simply share what has been shared with us to us to people who will receive what we have learned.

1 Peter 4:8-10 "Above all things have intense and unfailing love for one another, for love covers a multitude of sins [forgives and disregards the offenses of others]. Practice hospitality to one another (those of the household of faith). [Be hospitable, be a lover of strangers, with brotherly affection for the unknown guests, the foreigners, the poor, and all others who come your way who are of Christ's body.] And [in each instance] do it ungrudgingly (cordially and graciously, without complaining but as representing Him). As each of you has received a gift (a particular spiritual talent, a gracious divine endowment), employ it for one another as [befits] good trustees of God's many-sided grace [faithful stewards of the extremely diverse powers and gifts granted to Christians by unmerited favor]."

Journal

DAY SEVENTY EIGHT

Relationship "issues" are a perfect opportunity

I use to view people who were waiting on the Lord as passive. I always seem to think to myself "This person needs to do something" in regards to their circumstances. But after getting into loads of trouble for some of my own personal actions I am beginning to take a different view. Sowing to the "flesh" is giving into my own self efforts to "fix" what is wrong in my life. By trying to fix what is wrong I only make what is wrong worse.

One of the biggest lies taught to me was the lie that I had to deal with the problem lest it build up. The truth is that dealing with the problem only builds it up. This thinking led to self reliance. To sow to the spirit many times requires me to be silent before the Lord. But being silent alone isn't enough. I must lay myself down at the cross and be dominated by love. Spiritual examination must happen in the midst of my hardship. Yielding must happen at the moment of choice.

Sometimes to bring the Lord into our relationships require us to do nothing and just understand what happened at Calvary. Sometimes love endures without any action at all. Many times the Holy Spirit will bear long with life's circumstances, with us, and with others. When the occasion is right the Holy Spirit will find somebody who is open to the finished work of Christ to speak through.

If we were to ask ourselves "How am I following Christ's command to love others through Him?" We would have to also ask ourselves" How am I depending on the finished work of Christ and the work of the Holy Spirit?" Without the work of Christ's shed blood the commandment to love can be our greatest struggle. When we understand that He is love and we surrender to Him it takes the burden off us!

We have been freed from condemnation through the blood of Jesus Christ. Because of His death we now have His life. So we need to trust the Lord with our relationships. Without this trust our personal agenda can enter in. Our personal agenda involves our selfishness and our own efforts to get along with others. Without the forgiveness and patience of God we WILL see the behavior of others as offensive. We can become defensive when we feel that our needs are not being met by them. Then others react to our defenses and we set up walls. This is not the love of God! If we don't trust the Lord with our relationships we turn all our expectations onto others. We can make others or ourselves the object of our devotion. It's a form of idolatry. The payoff for placing this expectation on ourselves and others will always be negative.

1 Peter 5:4-6 "And [then] when the Chief Shepherd is revealed, you will win the conqueror's crown of glory. Likewise, you who are younger and of lesser rank, be subject to the elders (the ministers and spiritual guides of the church)--[giving them due respect and yielding to their counsel]. Clothe (apron) yourselves, all of you, with humility [as the garb of a servant, so that its covering cannot possibly be stripped from you, with freedom from pride and arrogance] toward one another. For God sets Himself against the proud (the insolent, the overbearing, the disdainful, the presumptuous, the boastful)--[and He opposes, frustrates, and defeats them], but gives grace (favor, blessing) to the humble. Therefore humble yourselves [demote, lower yourselves in your own estimation] under the mighty hand of God, that in due time He may exalt you"

Journal

DAY SEVENTY NINE

Sin. It is what it is!

By taking things into our own hands we are depending on our own useless efforts to solve the problems we face in our life. "Personal management" is the opposite of being managed by God. Self effort always equates to personal works. Personal works can lead to shortcomings and devastating sins. Character defects have severe consequences because sin always carries with it a dark condemnation of everything it touches. These consequences are never easily tolerated. Character defects are sin. It helps us greatly when we see character defects as sin along side with all its ugliness attached to it.

Calling character defects and shortcomings "sin" brings them into proper perspective. These sinful character defects are to be hated and not tolerated. This perspective brings into clarity the cure. The cure is Christ and Him crucified. The powers of all those sins were eliminated with Christ on His cross! The "shell game" over the meaning of words has to come to an end. Satan attempts to obscure the truth. We need to become more comfortable with the finished work of Christ than we are with our character defects.

The "flesh" is rarely spoken of. Why is that? It's one of our greatest enemies! We need an understanding that the "flesh" is our own efforts under the control of unbelief and fear. This is at the root of our sinful character defects. Bearing these sinful character defects is painful. We can release them to the work of the cross and experience relief from the burden of sin. It's all due to what Christ did at Calvary. He established our identity through His crucifixion and resurrection. Our only sin is rejecting Christ and the power of His blood in our current situation!

We have to discover these truths through personal research We need to let go of personal control and release our problems to God's control and ways of doing things. When we are not in a state of yielding we find ourselves in all kinds of trouble. Speaking the blood of Christ over our situation while at the same time understanding it's meaning brings evil to an end in many ways. Let's not let the words shortcomings and character defects minimize the destructive power of sin

1 John 1:6-8 "[So] if we say we are partakers together and enjoy fellowship with Him when we live and move and are walking about in darkness, we are [both] speaking falsely and do not live and practice the Truth [which the Gospel presents]. But if we [really] are living and walking in the Light, as He [Himself] is in the Light, we have [true, unbroken] fellowship with one another, and the blood of Jesus Christ His Son cleanses (removes) us from all sin and guilt [keeps us cleansed from sin in all its forms and manifestations].If we say we have no sin [refusing to admit that we are sinners], we delude and lead ourselves astray, and the Truth [which the Gospel presents] is not in us [does not dwell in our hearts]."

Journal

_____

_____

_____

_____

_____

_____

DAY EIGHTY

Sanctification and recovery

The scriptures suggest that we do not forsake assembling and sharing one another's burdens. Christians do need a place to go when they are facing sin and addiction problems. The worst thing they can do is isolate. This sin and addiction is something they need to get out in the open, discuss, and put behind them. Otherwise it will destroy their life as they know it and any hope to live a good life that lies ahead of them.

There is a need for Christians to meet in groups. Some of us have serious addiction problems and the consequences have become too devastating to bear. We needed something to help us out of our crushing dilemma but we had no idea where to go. But I need to make something clear. We need to experience sanctification more than recovery. Recovery is regaining control over our lives. We need more than control over our lives. We need to allow God to take control of our daily experience.

Most of us had tried 12 step meetings, pastoral counseling, psychotherapy, and some of us even tried psychiatric help. Most of us had tried devout prayer, church attending, and worship. Although some of these practices are a part of being a Christian there was still something missing.

We needed a place where we could share candidly in a group of other people who were nonjudgmental. We needed an accepting "family". We needed a place where we could experience true relationship and understanding. In this way we honor God. If we are Christians we are already sanctified in Christ but to experience it in our life requires faith in that fact. None of the methods stated above will work unless they point to the work that was done at the cross.

Hebrews 10:25 "Not forsaking or neglecting to assemble together [as believers], as is the habit of some people, but admonishing (warning, urging, and encouraging) one another, and all the more faithfully as you see the day approaching"

Journal_____

_____

_____

_____

_____

_____

_____

DAY EIGHTY ONE

Through the doors of a 12 step program

Many of us have come back to the church through the the doors of a 12 step program. We learned the importance of believing in, and deciding to live for God. We were reacting toward Gods love toward us. This ability to believe and choose was placed in us by God. We came to a point where we decided that we were no longer going to reject God and His plan for our life.

The reality is the fact that we are not created by ourselves! We are created by God to be in relationship with Christ. This seems simple enough but we find that our pride is very hard. The good news is that the blood of Christ is all powerful and stands eternal! The only bad decision we make is rejecting Christ and His shed blood as it relates to our current situation! The gift of life that we can have now is not earned.

Recovery for the born again believer and recovery for those who are not converted are very different. The terms "character defects" and "shortcomings" also have different meanings to the believer than the unbeliever. The un-converted have been taught by our society that they are inherently good. There is no need for the cross of Christ to recover. The Christian believes that change comes through Christ crucified and the forgiveness of the sin of unbelief.

Christ's blood brings us joy because we know it contains power. To the non-Christian it is just a gloomy thought Christians also see character defects and shortcomings as a result of the sin of unbelief. To those who are not born again it just means that they have some imperfections. Recovery to the person of the world means to get back everything they lost in this world. To us who have been totally restored "recovery" means to be brought back from a sinful lifestyle and to reclaim what satan has taken from us. This decision making process is guided by the Holy Spirit.

1 Peter 2:8-10 "And, A Stone that will cause stumbling and a Rock that will give [men] offense; they stumble because they disobey and disbelieve [God's] Word, as those [who reject Him] were destined (appointed) to do. But you are a chosen race, a royal priesthood, a dedicated nation, [God's] own purchased, special people, that you may set forth the wonderful deeds and display the virtues and perfections of Him Who called you out of darkness into His marvelous light. Once you were not a people [at all], but now you are God's people; once you were unpitied, but now you are pitied and have received mercy."

Journal

DAY EIGHTY TWO

Positive confessions to make in group

To make a confession is simply to make known a certain truth. But what kind of a confession is beneficial to make within our gatherings? We can share that it is our belief in Christ and our total faith in Him that initiates His ascendancy over us. We can share that His ascendancy over us not only includes our will but all the psychological and social aspects of ourselves as well. We can find the right words that fit for us as individuals to state this confession. We can share that when we totally yield ourselves in faith that we automatically have God's peace. We can share that He put to death the old man we were at His cross.

An accurate confession can also be centered in the new creation that was created in us at the cross and upon His resurrection. We can verbalize our insights into the difference between the fruitless works of self effort and the beneficial results of Christ crucified. These confessions will not only help other people it will also solidify our understanding. Understanding is necessary to experience the full benefits of what God has done for us. We share who He is, what He has done for us, and His love for us. When we do this we will be helping others to understand how to believe and trust in God for themselves. People need answers on how to live for God

Wherever we gather as Christians we are responsible to converse about Christ and what He did for us at the cross and how that contributes to our life or recovery. What He did for us at the cross was an expression of love. He didn't just save us from our sins at the cross. He also gave us a sanctified path to walk on. We can share the fact that we did not combat our addictions and sins on our own. We can share that Christ took care of our sin for us. We can share that our part was to lean on what He did for us and walk in faith. We can share the fact that our own independent self effort to become who we already were in Christ thwarted us.

We can share the fact that we were restored by Christ exclusively and regenerated. We can share how we did our inventory of what God has done for us and how we looked within for the faith that God had given us. We can share about how we looked within for acceptance of the truth and how we looked at our decisions and indecisions to trust God. We can share how we looked to see where we are sharing His love and where we rejecting Him. We can share how our bad behaviors, and also our attempts to do well on our own, were rooted in the demonic. We can share our understanding of our futile "attempts" to live this Christian life without God's grace. We can share our struggles but more importantly how Christ won our battles. Let us not waste the time we spend together. It's war out there!

We honestly share in our groups the reason why we come to these meetings. All of us are growing strong and have had our struggles with sin. Our growth and understanding is expanding and we need a place where we can articulate with some precision what is happening with us. This is along the lines of the principle of confession. Yes! We have a confession to make. It is more of a proclamation! Jesus has set us free! So we share publicly that we believe and that we have made a decision to allow Him to have His way in our lives. We gladly yield to what He has done for us! We shared that there came a time in our lives that we had to be honest with ourselves. Then there came a time when we had to stop focusing on ourselves. We had to choose to take advantage of the finished work of Christ in our lives. Not actively expressing our faith created in us spiritual passivity and complacency. So we share our faith actively. Let's share that faith in our Christian groups.

Hebrews 3:13 "But instead warn (admonish, urge, and encourage) one another every day, as long as it is called Today, that none of you may be hardened [into settled rebellion] by the deceitfulness of sin [by the fraudulence, the stratagem, the trickery which the delusive glamor of his sin may play on him]."

Journal_____

_____
_____
_____
_____
_____
_____
_____

DAY EIGHTY THREE

Self governing effort and a Spirit led obedience

This is one of the biggest lessons we all have to learn in our life. If we are complete in Christ and have been made new creations how are we to consider "sinful character defects" and "shortcomings"? The Christian has been made a new creation. This new man that we are was created without sinful character defects and shortcomings. Yet in our lives we find within ourselves sinful character defects and shortcomings. So we ask ourselves "How can this be?". The answer is that we create within ourselves sinful character defects and shortcomings when we take our eyes off Christ and His finished work at the cross. When we do this we place our eyes on ourselves, on others, or something else. This is actually fear motivated.

The deception is that we will be at a loss by doing Gods will. Then unbelief precedes independent behaviors and creates sinful character defects. To understand these sinful character defects we must draw a line between self governing effort and Spirit led obedience. Satan is forever pushing deception, fear and unbelief on us to engage us in self governing effort. This always leads to sin. What we need is spirit led obedience.

How does one live a life of spirit led obedience? It comes by listening to the words of the Holy Spirit in regards to living this Christian life. The Spirit beckons us to trust in how God operates. God operates through the laws of the new creation established in us at the cross! When we come to the end of ourselves it is no longer about sinful character defects. It is about how God is accomplishing His purposes in us. His love is found in the act of what he did at the cross. That same exact love that was expressed there by Him is now available in the same form here and now. Do you have insights into what happened to man there at the cross? May the Lord Himself increase this understanding and open wide your eyes.

Trusting in the blood of Christ must be complete lest we trust in ourselves. Self reliance is rooted in the worldly and in demonic influence. We are to rely on the Lord. Self reliance is a form of bondage to self. Human reasoning and self determination doesn't remove sin. As we come to know what Christ did for us at the cross our sinful "character defects" and "shortcomings" seem to fade away. Then we can say along with the Apostle Paul "The law of the freedom of life in Christ Jesus has set me free from the law of sin and death"!

1 John 3:10-12 "By this it is made clear who take their nature from God and are His children and who take their nature from the devil and are his children: no one who does not practice righteousness [who does not conform to God's will in purpose, thought, and action] is of God; neither is anyone who does not love his brother (his fellow believer in Christ). For this is the message (the an- nouncement) which you have heard from the first, that we should love one another, [And] not be like Cain who [took his nature and got his motivation] from the evil one and slew his brother. And why did he slay him? Because his deeds (activities, works) were wicked and malicious and his brother's were righteous (virtuous)"

Journal

DAY EIGHTY FOUR

The Christian choice

The temptation is to place our faith in something outside of the finished work Christ has accomplished for us. The big temptation in our society is to think that through introspection we can solve our problems. We know it's not a good idea to disregard the finished work of Christ and move on to another method of self improvement. We know this would be a grave mistake. There are methods of living that might mention Jesus and leave out the pathway through Christ's crucifixion and resurrection. The psychology book shelves are filled with them. These are most likely false teaching or as the scriptures call "another Jesus". We weigh every message by its "blood content" to see that it leans and points to Christ crucified as the solution. If it doesn't then the message is leaning else ware and is faulty.

The meeting of our own psychological and social needs through our own self reliance was not only a sin but also a bad habit. It was time for us to make the right kind of choice. We made a decision to abandon our methods of self control and to make ourselves available to the Lord. We understood that we have been baptized into Christ's death. Our old reasoning had to leave us. In Christ we are more than conquers because we died with Christ and rose with Him in His resurrection. This is where the principle of conversion takes place. The blood of Christ put a period mark on our sinful lifestyle. Self effort in regards to spiritual matters always results in failure. No matter how successful it appears, it is ungodly. Our choice is used to surrender to Gods way for us and we give Him our whole life to do with as He pleases. We are now making choices in ways we are not use to.

We are processing our choices upon the work of the cross. We are making our choices based on the moving of the Spirit in our lives. We now experience a different type of control in our lives. It is the fruit of the Spirit. We always keep in mind the finished work of Christ. We learned that the work that was done at the cross is constantly available for us to respond to in all the circumstances of our lives by the Holy Spirit.
Every principality and power was addressed by Christ at the cross. We know that placing our faith in what happened at the cross is the source of life.

Romans 6:3-6 "Are you ignorant of the fact that all of us who have been baptized into Christ Jesus were baptized into His death? We were buried therefore with Him by the baptism into death, so that just as Christ was raised from the dead by the glorious [power] of the Father, so we too might [habitually] live and behave in newness of life. For if we have become one with Him by sharing a death like His, we shall also be [one with Him in sharing] His resurrection [by a new life lived for God]. We know that our old (unrenewed) self was nailed to the cross with Him in order that [our] body [which is the instrument] of sin might be made ineffective and inactive for evil, that we might no longer be the slaves of sin."

Journal

DAY EIGHTY FIVE

His blood removes our defects

To have defects is not Gods intention for us. The cross and Christ's shed blood perfects us! Character defects are just sins that we commit due to our capacity to make bad choices. Let's not water it down and exchange the truth for a lie. These sins are removed by Christ's shed blood. He creates in us His perfection. It's not of our making. It is of His making. It's His perfection! Christ's commandments to love could not be fulfilled until the gift of the Holy Spirit within us was granted. It took Christ crucified in order for that to happen! His blood cleaned out a place in our heart for the Holy Spirit to reside.

Christ's commandments were given so "that ye should go and bring forth fruit". Fruit is of the Spirit. He has delivered us and He will continue to deliver us! All self sufficiency needs to come to an end. We need to place our hope in the finished work of Christ. His resurrection power is forever present for us and is the means of change and the elimination of evil! It's not about our will to change, it's about what the blood of Christ has accomplished

We gain perspective and an understanding of what Christ crucified and resurrected means to us. We are no longer who we use to be and the powers of our own efforts were broken there. The thinking that we surrender our innermost selves must change into the accepting of His life in us. There is a vast difference between the two. One is of God and one is of self! The main character defect is rebellion against God which leads to all other character defects. This rebellion is motivated by fear which is of darkness.

We don't even have what it takes to become entirely ready to have God remove our character defects. We need God every small step of the way. We need a savior. We need Him to do for us what we can not do for ourselves. Our salvation and sanctification does not depend on our capacity to be honest either. Our innermost self is not capable of being honest. Truth is given by revelation through God. It comes from accepting what Christ did for us at the cross. He sanctified us.

1 John 3:23-24 "And this is His order (His command, His injunction): that we should believe in (put our faith and trust in and adhere to and rely on) the name of His Son Jesus Christ (the Messiah), and that we should love one another, just as He has commanded us. All who keep His commandments [who obey His orders and follow His plan, live and continue to live, to stay and] abide in Him, and He in them. [They let Christ be a home to them and they are the home of Christ.] And by this we know and understand and have the proof that He [really] lives and makes His home in us: by the [Holy] Spirit Whom He has given us."

Journal

DAY EIGHTY SIX

A Christian does not just confess his wrongs.

There came a time when I found myself in Christian groups being prompted to dig deep and talk about my problems. I thought to myself "something is not right here". It seemed to be getting gloomier and gloomier as I attended these groups and only heard people going over and over the same problems and not seeming to get anywhere in their lives. So I took personal responsibility and started to focus on the positive contributions on Christ's finished work and how that could be related to our lives.

This began to have a positive effect on the group as a whole as others started to confess their victory in Christ! There will always be times of unmanageability, desperation, and a need to turn to the Lord in our lives. The closer you get to God the greater this need will become. Everything in our lives can turn into a good thing if we trust God completely. However, if we continue to lean on our own laurels the slogan "If nothing changes nothing changes" will become a reality in our lives! It's important to admit to God, others and ourselves the exact nature of our wrong.

The exact nature of our wrong will always be rooted in unbelief and a rejection of Christ. When we "confess" this it shows that we are no longer in denial over our situation and have come to a place of honesty. It is then we will get what we need from the lord and move on. Admitting our wrongs should not be a long drawn out process. It would please satan if he can keep our noses in the dirt. Confession should eventually move beyond just confessing our wrongs. Being able to articulate the meaning of what happened at the cross would be meaningful to both us and our group. We overcome as the scripture states "by the blood of the lamb and the word of our testimony"

When we share with precision the message of what happened to us at the cross we confirm our understanding of it. When we are able to share insight into how we were delivered from sin and addiction others can learn from our experience as well. We learned from Romans Chapter 7 that we are not designed to help ourselves. We learn this as we listen to the Apostle Paul describe what happened to him when he tried to live this life by the "law" under the power of his own effort. This attempt became ungodly for him. It is true for us as well.

All of us need to make a public confession of what we believe at one time or another. When we took a look at ourselves and we saw all the great things God has done for us to make us new creatures the next thing we wanted to do is share that truth with others so that they may find the same things for themselves. But we also found areas where we were not trusting Christ with our lives completely. We needed to share these things as well so that we could receive prayer and counsel. It's a biblical approach to do so.

Where do we share these things? Good friends in a Christian group offer the perfect setting. Christian groups are not ordinary groups of people. We have a very well defined method for change and living. Successful groups require a dependency on God and the finished work of Christ for their strength. It is a place where God can deliver His message to us. In our groups we can connect with others and grow spiritually. We can talk about our experience of yielding to the work of God in our hearts!

1 John 4:6-8 "We are [children] of God. Whoever is learning to know God [progressively to perceive, recognize, and understand God by observation and experience, and to get an ever-clearer knowledge of Him] listens to us; and he who is not of God does not listen or pay attention to us. By this we know (recognize) the Spirit of Truth and the spirit of error. Beloved, let us love one another, for love is (springs) from God; and he who loves [his fellowmen] is begotten (born) of God and is coming [progressively] to know and understand God [to perceive and recognize and get a better and clearer knowledge of Him]. He who does not love has not become acquainted with God [does not and never did know Him], for God is love."

Journal

DAY EIGHTY SEVEN

A "Christian" inventory will reveal that we are new creations

As we do our inventories also keep in mind that our baptism in Christ although a one time event objectively is many times wrongly viewed as a one time event subjectively. It is an ongoing daily event and the "means" of living the Christian life experientially. Likewise the blood of Christ washed away our sin objectively. It also washes away our sins subjectively. The blood of Christ keeps our sins washed away daily according to our faith in Christ's death, burial, and resurrection. The blood holds us up righteously in the most adverse circumstances. This goes way beyond just changing our thoughts to be "more Godly". Let us immerse our minds and our life in the reality of redemption.

The saying that "If it's going to be it's up to me" is a dangerous code to live by. It's really not our job to correct ourselves psychologically and socially. If we could do this then why would we need to be connected to the Lord? The use of other "means" outside of our baptism into Christ can only cause us damage. However, that is the choice God gives us! Human reasoning has little to do with bringing about the changes that is needed in our lives. Psychology teaches us to focus on our thoughts to improve our lives. This is an incomplete truth. Our thoughts automatically come into the truth as we understand Gods plan for living our lives through what Christ did for us at the cross by shedding His blood. Our focus is to be on the finished work of Christ and how His victory over satan applies to our daily living.

It's not about the changing of our thoughts to make us feel better. Focusing on changing our thoughts without a complete dependency on what Christ did for us is deception. It promises fulfillment while avoiding Gods solution for us. Our attachment to His blood, His crucifixion, His resurrection, and His love is what changes us. Attempting to fix the psychological and social aspects of ourselves while at the same time excluding God could be based in darkness. Our character defects in these areas are just symptoms of a lack of faith. God must be fully considered when we look at these areas of our lives. It is in Him that the solution exists. There are many opinions on how to have successful relations and thinking. But Gods ways are not mans ways. We must keep this in mind. The Holy Spirit lives in us because the blood of Christ cleanses out a place for Him. It is not accomplished on our own.

1 John 4:10-13 "In this is love: not that we loved God, but that He loved us and sent His Son to be the propitiation (the atoning sacrifice) for our sins. Beloved, if God loved us so [very much], we also ought to love one another. No man has at any time [yet] seen God. But if we love one another, God abides (lives and remains) in us and His love (that love which is essentially His) is brought to completion (to its full maturity, runs its full course, is perfected) in us! By this we come to know (perceive, recognize, and understand) that we abide (live and remain) in Him and He in us: because He has given (imparted) to us of His [Holy] Spirit."

Journal

DAY EIGHTY EIGHT

More on Christian groups

Those who are in recovery know about sinful character defects. Our lifestyle caused damage to others and ourselves. But now we depend on and trust what Christ did for us at the cross for restoration. It was there that He was crucified, buried and resurrected as and for us! It was His blood that cleansed us and keeps us clean. This is what restores us to sanity! This is our confession.

Christian groups are an excellent forum to share and testify of our personal cuciformed and resurrected experience in Christ. It is there that we can proclaim our victories in Christ. We can share what we've learned about our regeneration and restoration process. We can also share how admitting to a problem, believing in the Lord, making good choices, and seeing ourselves from Gods perspective has changed our lives.

We acknowledge the fact that focusing on getting our needs met on our own only frustrated us. We can share that we learned that this frustration is a symptom of not trusting in the Lord. We can share the fact that now we know that on the spiritual level Christ worked out all our issues at the cross. It is there that He destroyed our affiliation with darkness and replaced it with His light. We share that it is our belief in this fact and our obedience to the Spirit that carries out His will for us.

Groups are a place for studying and honest sharing. It is there that we can address personal issues socially. Are we close to the Lord? Are we rebelling against Him? Are we experiencing belief or are we experiencing unbelief? Do we feel that we are using our will properly or are we misusing our will? We are instructed by Gods word to encourage one another and also to confess our sins to one another. Honestly sharing with our Christian family can bring these things to the light. However, confession without a bearing on the work of Christ's cross and His blood shed is unproductive.

Ephesians 4:15-17 "Rather, let our lives lovingly express truth [in all things, speaking truly, dealing truly, living truly]. Enfolded in love, let us grow up in every way and in all things into Him Who is the Head, [even] Christ (the Messiah, the Anointed One). For because of Him the whole body (the church, in all its various parts), closely joined and firmly knit together by the joints and ligaments with which it is supplied, when each part [with power adapted to its need] is working properly [in all its functions], grows to full maturity, building itself up in love. So this I say and solemnly testify in [the name of] the Lord [as in His presence], that you must no longer live as the heathen (the Gentiles) do in their perverseness [in the folly, vanity, and emptiness of their souls and the futility] of their minds."

Journal

_____

_____

_____

_____

_____

_____

DAY EIGHTY NINE

Gods love communicates perfectly

When I first came into recovery some years ago I had a lot of cleaning up to do. I had to make an amends for the destructive behavior I engaged in when I was active in my addiction. Apologies were in order. I had to compensate the best way I could for injuries that I inflicted. Nowadays it's all about preventing injuries toward others by avoiding being unjust and indifferent. Dealing with difficult people has been a challenge. I found myself to be at the top of the list. Many times I've sat out to improve my relationships and to "get along" with others. I have found out through endless hardships that this is not an endeavor to be accomplished by me alone. The way to love one another is through Christ! I have to look to Him to be in the center of my relationships. If I don't look to Christ and the new creation He created in me at His cross I can easily fall prey to the bitterness of the flesh. The bitterness of the flesh is an enemy of mine. It quickly escalates to anger. I fail miserably if I focus on mine or another's social behavior and attempt to fix those behaviors on my own. I need to see myself and others by looking at the spiritual. Due to the blood of Christ I can see other Christians and even myself as a saint! And all the glory goes to God!

It is not until we understand the Lords position in regards to our sinful character defects that we can understand how it applies to others. We will come to an understanding that it is Christ alone that cares for us and others. It is Him alone that can make us complete. We on our own have no defense. But, if we claim the blood we have all the power in the universe. He loves us all and has made us all kings and priests. We in turn give all the glory to Him. To do this we need to understand how we are relieved of self centeredness through Christ's cross. We will also need to come to believe that God can do for others through us what we can not do for them on our own! But this will require us to take what is irritating us to the Lord. Only the Lord can meet this expectation that we are placing on this other person to meet for us. As we allow the Lord to put us to rest with ourselves then that rest is passed on. When I feel that others are rubbing me the wrong way that is a pretty good indicator that I am in a selfish state. This is the area where Christ's death unto sin works toward my advantage. His death UNTO sin opens up the way of love. His death and resurrection combined gives me the freedom that I need to be guided by the Holy Spirit.

Relationships can become very difficult and without a doubt are life's greatest challenges. It's when we neglect to trust God with our difficult relationships that we find ourselves spiritual mishandling others. Unfortunately when we lack God's love and patience for others we have a tendency to injure others emotionally. It is important for us to be able to detect those "slight" words and actions that hurt and offend others. We can detect our misconduct because we are convicted of the Holy Spirit to share God's love and longsuffering. When we hurt others we need to admit to ourselves and to the lord that somehow we've escaped His grace. We admit when we have violated the patience that is due to our Christian brothers and sisters. The scriptures state that we are to bear one another and to forgive one another. It also states that if we have a quarrel against anybody that we are to forgive as Christ has forgiven. We can only do this if we factor in the finished work of Christ into the equation.

We are not to take up vengeance toward others. In other words we are to let go of spitefulness and disengage from perpetuating a destructive relationship. When we understand that Christ has set us free from our sinful character defects we will be in a greater position to allow the Lord to use us to extend this grace to others. The cross of Christ puts to end evil. Christ came to take away the sin of the world. He lives in our hearts. We are unable to hide the light that is within us! Making an estimation of ourselves or others outside of Gods frame of reference of Christ's shed blood causes major character defects in ourselves and can contribute to the defects of others. It complicates the freedom that is found in Christ. Because of the shed blood of Christ we can see one another as innocent children even though sometimes it may seem we are not! When we encounter the love of God we encounter it for ourselves as well as for others.

Ephesians 5:15-17 "Look carefully then how you walk! Live purposefully and worthily and accurately, not as the unwise and witless, but as wise (sensible, intelligent people), Making the very most of the time [buying up each opportunity], because the days are evil. Therefore do not be vague and thoughtless and foolish, but understanding and firmly grasping what the will of the Lord is."

Journal

DAY NINETY

Keep coming back!

The love of God can carry us through rough times in our relationships. Love is patient and does not rejoice in evil. Even though we judge evil actions as such, we are not in the position to set ourselves up to judge others or to express condemnation. It damages us as well as them. If we allow the sin of another to place us in judgment it leads to self righteousness. Being offended can only cause a division. We must keep in mind that God valued this person enough to die for them as well as for us. At a very deep level God accepts everyone as they are. So our relationships with others require a call on the Lord. He places us in relationship. Now we need Him so that we are not set off track through our interactions with people. It is required of us to rest in the finished work of Christ and then wait for the Holy Spirit to bring the fruit we so desperately need. The Holy Spirit brings the fruit of love. It is not self generated. The sin that I commit is not allowing Christ to enter my relationships.

When we came into our Christian gatherings we knew God would change us because of what we were hearing from other group members. We heard others share about their problems with sin and how they found a way out. Finally a light shined on the path in front of us. We were not exactly sure how the change was going to occur in us at first. However, we heard the promises being given to us by others who walked paths similar to ours. We finally heard the voice of the Lord through others who have had similar experience to ours. It was in our groups we heard that we were made new and set free by what happened at Christ's cross. What we had found was a gathering of people who had discovered an approach to deliver the message to us. People who were sharing a solution to their problems. People who were also sharing their struggles if they had struggles. People who were genuine and without pretence. People with transparency who shared their faith in God in ways that made sense to us. We heard that the solution was in Christ and the person He created us to be!

It was here that we were reminded that salvation and sanctification come as a gift from God. Salvation is freedom from sin and its penalty. Sanctification is a holy path set out before us from God. There is nothing we can do to earn our salvation or our sanctification. These come through what happened at the cross of Christ only. We were reminded that it wasn't the group itself that changed us and only the personhood of the Lord Himself could set us free. Even though we were attending a man made program we were cautious not to put too much faith in a "program". An attempt to overuse a program is to make an idol out of the program, to exchange addictions to a "program" addiction, or make recovery a legalistic approach. We don't serve the created we serve The Creator. A good program is designed not to cause dependence on the program but dependency on the one who can free us. The savior and sanctifier is Jesus Christ. Without a bearing on the cross of Christ a group can be elevated above its intended purpose and "worked" legalistically with the purpose of receiving Gods grace. We remember that we are recovered because we were regenerated by the work of the cross alone and made new.

Jude 1:3 "Beloved, my whole concern was to write to you in regard to our common salvation. [But] I found it necessary and was impelled to write you and urgently appeal to and exhort [you] to contend for the faith which was once for all handed down to the saints [the faith which is that sum of Christian belief which was delivered verbally to the holy people of God]."

Journal

_____

_____

_____

_____

_____

_____

_____

_____

Additional Notes:

Made in the USA
Lexington, KY
11 September 2011